Im

the
Possibilities

A Conversation with Graduates

Mark and Sara Welshimer

Copyright © 2006
Mark Welshimer

All rights reserved. No part of this book may be reproduced in any
form, except for the inclusion of brief quotations in a review,
without permission in writing from the author or publisher.

ISBN: 0-9785615-0-3

Library of Congress Control Number: 2006903533

Printed in the United States by:
Morris Publishing
3212 East Highway 30
Kearney, NE 68847
1-800-650-7888

Foreword

Much of what we have compiled comes from many years of seeing hundreds of students graduate and go on to lead wonderfully successful lives. From being their youth minister, teacher, Sunday School Teacher, mentor and friend, we have some wisdom we would like to pass on to you. As the passing of the years never seem to cease, it breaks our hearts every time we have to say goodbye to another graduating class. However, the anticipation of wonderful things to come in your life makes us smile and perhaps even gives us hope.

Heart knowledge is a path to help you be a more well-rounded person. While head knowledge is valuable for learning skills, ideas and structures that will help you in the future, true heart knowledge engages your whole being. We hope as you begin to mature, you not only seek, but have a real passion for heart knowledge. We want you to know the truth that further propels you to a principled way of life. So that it can spurn you on to a successful, productive, effective and happy future.

Mark shares principles of living while Sara shares stories about her relationships with seniors *(names and some conversations have been recreated in order to protect the identities of individuals)*. The basis of this book is from *2 Peter 1:3-8*. We believe this text has a great outline of profound ideas that can communicate meaningful themes for our day, especially for graduates. These four key principles can unlock the secrets of success: divide, subtract, add, multiply. They are simple to begin, yet take a lifetime to master. As you continue your journey to the next phase of life, we hope you take some of these morsels of truth and embed them into your souls. So when push comes to shove, these helpful life suggestions which reside in your soul will summon you to mighty, courageous and heroic living where you can imagine the possibilities.

Contents

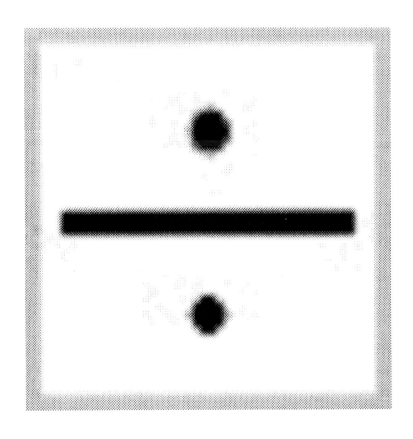

His divine power has given us everything we need for life and godliness through our knowledge of him who called us by his own glory and goodness.   *2 Peter 1:3*

DIVIDE... Make your life full!

What makes life full? As you graduate, one of the best principles you can learn to make life full is the principle of division. You might hear people say, "These years will be some of the best times of your lives, so live your life to the fullest..." but how do you do that? "The thief comes only to steal, kill, and destroy, but Jesus came that you might have life and have it to the full" *(John 10:10)*. This passage suggests a "robber" who perpetrates dastardly deeds that not only take away from life, but also do harmful damage. If you have ever been robbed, you know how this feels. Someone stole something from you, violated trust, looked through stuff and maybe even personally hurt you. Many people live life as if their happiness, success and future were already robbed. God, however, came to give life to the fullest to those who would trust in Him. Full life is His divine power to help us survive and succeed in our daily lives. So the foundation of building a full life starts with a simple trust in God.

God desires us to make our lives full by dividing the bigger picture into smaller pieces. When we work on the smaller, sometimes more manageable pieces, the bigger picture becomes more full. Jigsaw puzzles are fascinating. At conception, it seems like total chaos when all the pieces are spread out. As the organizing process begins, the straight-edged sides start to take shape. Once the border is complete, the middle fills in, with similar shapes, colors and designs. The focus is on one area for a while, strenuously searching for pieces that might connect with each other. Little by little, one piece at a time, the puzzle is filled. The concept is the same when climbing mountains. At first, the summit seems far away, but it can be conquered, one step at a time.

Divide by focusing... Division helps focus on smaller areas of the bigger picture, to give the whole depth, weight and fullness. Alcoholics Anonymous knows the value of division. When a person decides to quit using, AA does not tell the user that he/she can never use again. This may cause the user to become overwhelmed which results in immediately seeking to medicate or binge one last time. Instead, the user considers "one day at a time" which means "what happened in the past is over, and while I can't control the future, today I'll stay clean and sober." Dividing addiction makes conquering it manageable. This helps the addict focus on one day at a time. Universities divide a well-rounded education into years, semesters, classes, tests and assignments. For the student to excel, he/she must focus on one class at a time and give merit to each grade and assignment. Class builds upon class, semester upon semester, and the outcome is a solid education built one class at a time. Divide in order to build something that will last.

The biggest project for senior year is the infamous Research Paper. Teachers spend a lot of time explaining the process, and students spend a lot of time actually writing. The problem is this: there is always at least one person per class that has a hard time writing and does not get his or her paper done. One day late turns into one week, which turns into two weeks, which turns into... well, you get the picture. This year it was Jason. He was so nervous about writing his paper his mother called and said he was close to quitting school! I called Jason in. "Just do the paper," I said. "I'm worried it won't be correct!" he explained. "How will you know unless it gets done? Let me tell you the story of two students. One is a great writer. She writes beautiful sentences intertwined with her own style that will one day create the perfect essay. There is another student who is an okay writer. He focuses on completing the paper. Guess which one graduates? The second one." "What?" he asked quizzically. "The second student finished his paper and actually turned it in. The first is still trying to get her paper perfect. That's why she failed and had to take the class again because she didn't graduate!" Jason turned his paper in the next week.

<u>Divide by knowing</u>... Know that "all things are yours" *(1 Corinthians 3:22).* In life, there are not many exhaustible commodities, but there is plenty of almost everything to go around. The only exhaustible commodity is time. Time can never be retrieved. Everything else is negotiable. Claim the promise of God: "All things are yours!" Teenagers in high school tend to view popularity as a scarce resource. If a rival student is popular, no one else can shine.

The "*Sibling Syndrome*" is where one sibling might receive the love of his/her parents, while the other siblings feel there is not enough love to go around. This seems to make a parent's love unattainable. In the Old Testament, Esau and Jacob *(Genesis 27:1-40)* struggled with each other for the blessing of their father before they made peace between themselves. In the Parable of the Prodigal Son *(Luke 15:11-32),* the older son is perturbed when he finds out his father was celebrating the return of the younger son who squandered his inheritance in wild living. It was the father who had to bring the older son back, as he reminded him, "My son… everything I have is yours." When this detrimental view of competitive family life spills into other areas of our lives, we feel defeated. We can not win or succeed at anything, because someone else has all the success. Do not buy into that lie. Learn the need to understand the secret of division. If this principle is learned, it will help not to view life as being either a have or have-not, but as a person who has the potential to have all things!

God has given us all things... "He who did not spare his own Son, but gave Him up for us all—how will He not also, along with Him, graciously give us all things?" *(Romans 8:32).* When opposition is met, know everything is yours. Everything God has created is good *(1 Timothy 4:4).* The promise "The earth is the Lord's, and everything in it…" *(Psalm 24)* means everything is available to us to make our lives full. God has given us everything we need for life and Godliness.

Some people interpret this principle to the materialism or celebrity myth: possessions or fame will make full lives. God, however, is more interested in the inward eternal values than the outward temporal stuff. **God wants to bless us spiritually** *(Ephesians 1:3),* and He wants us to depend upon Him for everything. He does not, however, want us to treat Him like a genie, butler or waitress. One year our Youth Ministry took a

Mission Trip to Mexico, and it was such an eye-opener for many students. In our "rat-race" society students feel like the luxuries of life are necessities. We sometimes lose perspective. We were in the poorer part of Mexico, where the people had no air-conditioning *(it was hot!),* no cell phones, no suv's, no plasma TV's and no computers. While some of these people did not even have a solid roof over their heads, clean water or a pantry of sanitary food, they were happy. Some were much happier than a lot of our students. Why? Their lives were full, and they reminded us of a valuable lesson Jesus taught: "Watch out! Be on your guard against all kinds of greed; a person's life does not consist in the abundance of their possessions" *(Luke 12:15).* If you ever start getting sad, depressed, unhappy or feel like you have nothing, go on a mission trip to an impoverished nation. See how the people live. Some of the happiest people live life to the fullest, even with so little resources! The secret is to count your blessings and learn how to enjoy what you have. Recognize the joy that is beyond circumstantial joy and experience more of an abiding presence of peace in your heart.

Every year for my birthday, I throw myself a party in my classes. We usually bring sweets, eat, and have a fun day. One year, Joel Emory would not eat any of the sweets even though he swore he ate brownies as his only sustenance at times. Students in the class asked him why. He explained he and his family were fasting for his brother. "My brother has really gotten himself badly into drugs, and so my family is fasting and praying for him this week." The class was in awe. "You can't eat anything?" one girl asked. "Why would you want to do something like that?" someone else asked. He was not embarrassed or upset. He just matter-of-factly told us he could not eat anything. "I want to fast because I want to do something to help my brother—but there is really nothing I can do. So, I am praying about it and leaving it in God's hands." His non-action spoke louder than any action he could have taken.

Divide by being content... Contentment is wealth. Paul learned the value of being content no matter his circumstances: "I know what it is to be in need, and I know what it is to have plenty. I have learned the secret of being content in any and every situation, whether well fed or hungry, whether living in plenty or in want" *(Philippians 4:12)*. Paul rested and trusted in the promise God would provide: "And my God will meet all of your needs according to His glorious riches in Christ Jesus" *(Philippians 4:19)*. In Proverbs, Agur asked God, "...give me neither poverty nor riches, but give me only my daily bread" *(Proverbs 30:8)*. Contentment is not found in desiring a lot of stuff we think may make us happy, but it is found in desiring the eternal things that will satisfy and yield life to the full.

Divide your finality... What are you doing with your time? If you knew this was your last year, week or day to live, how would you live differently? "Our lives are but a mist..." *(James 4:14)* is a great picture of the brevity of life. Hopefully, this will captivate our souls and ignite in us a passion to cherish and revere our remaining time on earth. Once we begin to understand the fleeting nature of life, it can capsize us as it brings us down to the abyss of wasted time. Or, it can catapult us into effective and escalated levels of living where we breach momentous experiences of life. There is value in understanding quality of life vs. quantity of life. "The length of our days is seventy years—or eighty, if we have the strength; yet their span is but trouble and sorrow, for they quickly pass, and we fly away... Teach us to number our days aright, that we may gain a heart of wisdom" *(Psalm 90:10-12)*. What are you doing with the quantity of your time? At what quality are you living your life? Your time is one of the most precious assets you will have, so spend it wisely. Realize your finality! Spend your life for something of value of which you can be proud. Go on trips. Serve others. Engage in new experiences. Do something valuable with your time.

How do you make your life full by dividing your time? Be early. Whether it is going to class, a meeting, work or play, arrive a few minutes early so you will not have to rush around, stressing out at the last minute. Organize a schedule with your calendar. This can be a visible reminder in order to see in advance what is coming up: important dates, tests and homework due dates. Be prepared to take the steps to achieve your goals. Keep a journal of activities so you can look back and reflect on your week, month, even year, remembering the good and challenging times. Use "down time" to discover life! Take your time. Do not rush through life. Do not "grow up" too fast, but as the old saying goes, "Take time to stop and smell the roses." Ask yourself at the end of each day, "How have I used my time today?" "What have I done eternally today?" Divide your time into work, play, fellowship, service, family, television and traveling.

Maximize your time by making the most of your minutes. If you are going to college, you are going there to study and learn. Discover your maximizing and most effective quality, not quantity, time to study. My first year of college, I planned on studying during the day and "playing" at night. I would sit in the library trying to read, looking at the same ten pages over and over, not retaining anything. I wasted a lot of time trying to study effectively during the day. After weeks of this ineffective schedule, I had to do something. I started studying at night. I discovered my peak time for effective studying was from 10:00 pm - 3:00 am. It was during these late night study times I could really focus, learn, retain knowledge and read faster. It is not how much time you spend studying that gets you a good grade, but the actuality of learning the material. What would take me four hours during the day, only took me one hour at night. You might be an early morning person, a late night owl or a daytime pro. Whoever you are, find what timetable works best for you.

My first period class was always behind my other classes, but I could not figure out why. I teach English IV all day—the same thing over and over again for five periods. So, by the fourth or fifth time, the stories we read can either get boring or more exciting. I looked at my schedule and I was arriving ten minutes before school started. I wrote any notes that had to be on the board. I counted my papers for a

quiz. I recorded yesterday's grades, and even had to read through a selection we were covering that day. So when first period actually started working, it was a good thirty minutes into the hour... more than half-way through the period. I discovered this was the reason why my first period was always behind! So, for a week, I decided to try something—I got to work thirty minutes earlier, and it made a great difference! First period was not behind that week! Not only did it give me time to prepare for class, it gave me an opportunity to talk to each of my students in first period and get to know them. I was less stressed because I was ready for the day to begin and was more confident of my ability to teach because I had been through the material already! Wow—what being a little early will do! Now when first period is behind, it is not because I just arrived, but that we were all too busy talking to do our work!

Divide your friends... Develop yourself as you learn to relate to a variety of diverse people. You need friends, and they need you *(Ecclesiastes 4:12).* Spend meaningful time with friends, and let their people be your people *(Ruth 1:16).* While it is true if you "run with dogs you may get fleas," God does not call Christians to run and hide from the world or the relationships it has to offer. Some Christians are so afraid of the world they do not have any non-Christian friends. God does not call us to sever ties with the world, but He tells us not to be yoked or totally influenced by it *(2 Corinthians 6:14).* God calls Christians to be as valuable as salt *(Matthew 5:13),* primarily through individual, influential relationships. How do you make your life full by dividing your friends and making your relationships influential? **If you want friends, be a friend first** *(1 John 3:16).* Jesus challenged us to not only love those who love us, as the tax collectors were doing, but also to love all people, even our enemies *(Matthew 5:44 & 46).* Respect precedes relationships. Relationships precede sharing your life with others. Sharing your life precedes sharing the Gospel. Sharing the Gospel precedes the acceptance of the Good News.

In other words, they will not listen to you unless they respect you first.

Do not be afraid to make new friends, especially if they are different than you. Remember you have **the light of the world** *(Matthew 5:14)* in your heart, and God wants to shine in the dark places of life. When I went to college, I decided to venture out, find new relationships and be and do something different. I started with a social fraternity. My Christian friends advised me against it. They told me it would be my downfall because "Bad company corrupts good character" *(1 Corinthians 15:33).* Instead of believing I was compromising and selling out my values to the world, I viewed myself as a missionary. I desired to take the light of Christ into the dark places of this world, and on my campus, the fraternal system seemed like a dark place that needed a little light. My first year, I would go to parties, retreats *(sometimes as the designated driver)* and be involved without having to go overboard as some of my friends did. As I got to know them better, I felt more comfortable about sharing my faith from the heart. They were more comfortable accepting it. As brothers, they witnessed my strong and weak times, but because I had an established relationship with them, they saw and appreciated the authenticity of my faith.

My first year of seminary, my roommate moved in with few articles of clothing and a couple of books. Within minutes, he divulged he was fresh out of serving nine years in prison! He tried to assure me, "Don't worry. I didn't go in for a violent crime, but for dealing drugs." I secretly thought, "How am I going to live with this guy?" but said, "sounds great!" As it turned out, we became the best of friends. He helped me learn about the small pleasures in life only a free person can experience, which I had taken for granted for so long. Do not be afraid to make friends, especially those with whom you think you might not like. Sometimes the most unlikely people can turn out to be just what you need.

John Reagan was so excited. He was given the part of "Osberon" in *Midsummer Night's Dream*. Most guys would be embarrassed to wear tights in front of their classmates.

**Most guys would not like the title "King of the Fairies."
Most guys would never flit around the stage dancing with a
bunch of girls, but not John. John was excited about it—and
he let everyone know! "I am he – the King of the Fairies," he
announced as he came into the room, and then twirled some
random girl around and danced a ballet-like number. You
would think some people would be embarrassed to have a
guy like this as a friend, but not John's friends! John's best
friends were big basketball players and student council
members. John's buddies were excited for him. They
enjoyed the fact he celebrated his uniqueness and they were
open to seeing a play with their best friend dancing, wearing
tights and being the "King of the Fairies."**

In relationships, sometimes you lead and sometimes you
follow. In healthy relationships, sometimes you influence, and
sometimes you are influenced. In your friendships, when are you
influenced or are you the influencer? Either can be both good
and/or bad at different times. But with whomever you choose to
associate, be open and inclusive, because you never know who
might become your best friend. As you consider your
friendships, they might each fall into one of these categories: (a)
Tolerance - A friend who has an idea different or opposed from
you, even after you have deciphered it is not truth. Once you
honestly decide it is not, you agree to disagree without being
disagreeable, while still maintaining the friendship. Do not
exclude your friend because he/she is different, but learn to
engage her/him without selling out your personal point of view.
Remember, whenever two people come together, each will have
differing opinions and interests. (b) Compromise – Give and
take with a friend, without hurting feelings or holding grudges.
Compromise because you enjoy the company and attempt to
understand each other for the sake of the friendship. (c)
Subscription – Change and subscribe your point of view to a
friend's point of view. You may choose to become like those
around you because they may make you a better person by
simply being around them.

When asked what employers are looking for in potential employees, many of them assert "teamwork" and "relating to other people" are common denominators in those they desire to hire. Learn to relate to a wide variety of people in various circumstances. You can always find something in common with someone if you try hard enough and discern your friendships by division. Just as every snowflake is unique and everyone has a different set of fingerprints, imagine how diverse humanity is: optimists, pessimists, doomsayers, prozacs, intellectuals, politicians, social economists and disciplinarians. Imagine the full gamut of emotions, intellect, spirituality, sexuality, family structure, race and even worldviews. Even religion has variety, especially within denominations and churches. Consider the diverse people from different parts of your city, state, country, and even the world. How will you relate to these various types of people, if they are your new co-workers, teammates, bosses, colleagues, sons or daughters? Learn to relate and be relatable, even with people with whom you seem to have nothing in common. You can always find some kind of common ground.

My class was having a discussion about sexual pressures that teenagers face (as an introduction to *Hamlet*). A student in my class, Mike, shared how difficult it was to be a virgin among his peers. "Everyone laughs at me behind my back because I have chosen to stay pure for my wife." That really got the class talking! As I was struggling to get the focus back, a popular girl named Shawna, who usually was quiet, spoke up. "I think more people would respect that decision than you realize. I was in a relationship for two years and I decided to stay pure for my husband and that was okay with my boyfriend." Several others in class voiced their decisions to stay pure even though their friends were not, but they refused to be ostracized for it. Mike and Shawna are perfect examples of students living in the world but setting themselves apart from it by their decisions.

College is a melting pot of all kinds of people. I had several different roommates—the most challenging was Katie. I went to bed at 10:00 pm; Katie was a night owl and went to bed at 4:00 am every night. I was a neat freak; Katie was a little messy. I did not like people touching my things; Katie thought she had equal access to everything in our room. Needless to say, we had to create boundaries on our things, our messes and especially our time. She promised to leave the room every night at 10:00 pm and stay gone until she was ready to go to sleep, as long as I was quiet in the morning when I got up so she could sleep in. She limited her mess to her bed and if I wanted to clean any area, I could put anything of hers on her bed, and she would be okay with that. She promised if she used anything of mine she would either replace it right away or put it back on the spot—compromise made us great roommates! To avoid moving around every semester, we had to learn to live with each other. I was sad when she eventually transferred to be closer to her boyfriend.

Divide your family… Friends, schools and jobs may come and go, but family is what stays and sticks throughout the years. They define who you are and will still be your family no matter where you go or what you do. Therefore, how you treat them matters. In family, there are good times and bad times, with unique dynamics between spouses, siblings, parents, grandparents, cousins, in-laws, steps, as well as the addition and loss of family members. Families sometimes get along and sometimes fight. Do not think it is any different for you when you have a family quarrel. The first fight was between brothers *(Genesis 4)*!

Your family has a heritage and a story, and you are a part of that story. Consider your genes, your upbringing, the rules of your house and the occupations of some of your family. Faith is usually imparted to children *(2 Timothy 1:5)*. What are you going to do with what you have been given? What faith has been imparted to you? What is your family story?

14

Students, as they embark on their epic journey from adolescence to adulthood, need to "break" from their authority figures, often called parents. As children, we believe what our parents believe, but as we grow up during the pubescent years, we start to learn and think for ourselves *(1 Corinthians 13:11)*. Students have to challenge and test rules, ideas and upbringings in order to draw conclusions for themselves. Sometimes it is a defining moment while other times it is a gradual change. Some do this in a graceful way without making too many waves, and others jaggedly rebel against everything that has been taught and given them. As you make this "break" and become your own man or woman, remember your parents are people too. They are vulnerable and can get their feelings hurt just like any other person! Sometimes, the people we love the most we hurt the most.

While Lily Thomas was an average student, she was funny and a really good trumpet player. She was failing, not only in my class, but also in two others she needed in order to graduate. She and I, along with another teacher and her principle, Mr. Grant, were called for a parent conference. In the meeting, we all expressed our concern for Lily and what she was and was not doing, what she needed to do and how we could individually help her achieve success in our classes. To my chagrin and complete horror, her father exploded in front of us all. "Lily, I can't believe you are such a failure! Your looks aren't going to get you anywhere, being so overweight and homely looking, and now you won't even have a high school degree! You might as well drop out of school and get a job at McDonald's! You are the epitome of loser!" She was as small as a fly. I wanted to wrap her up in my arms and love her. Did her dad not realize things did not come as easily for her as it did for others? Had he ever spent more than ten minutes talking to her and hearing her funny way of telling how she would go about mundane things? Had he never heard her play the trumpet? Had he ever just held her and told her he loved her? Mr. Grant put an end to the meeting and any further humiliation Lily's father may have

15

had for Lily. **From that day on, I tried my hardest to shower her with affection and praise.** She took her father's words and instead of allowing those words to bring her down, she rose above them. **She graduated from high school and went on to college with a scholarship for playing the trumpet. She is about to graduate with honors.** She wants to be a teacher in order to encourage students that may not otherwise be encouraged. **Oh, and she wants to be a mother. She says she will love her kids with everything in her no matter what they look or act like. I believe her.**

As you graduate, do not be afraid to move on. The first years, you might see your parents a lot. But, as the years go by, you might begin to see less and less of them, usually a day here or there turns into weeks here and there. You might become less and less dependent upon them, and more and more independent. But do not stop there. Become interdependent. In your independence, you can willfully depend on your parents and they upon you, because you need your family! When the hurricanes hit the Gulf in 2005, most people had to stay with family or go to a shelter. I will take family any day. As the old saying goes, "Blood is thicker than water."

The Scriptures give great guidelines in how to treat parents: "Honor your father and mother..." *(Ephesians 5:21-6:4)*. The first word that begins this passage, however, is "submit." Submit in order to honor your family members. Sounds easier than it is. To submit to family along with the complexities of life, in the midst of long-term relationships, let your family time be the time of "Jubilee." In the Old Testament, every 50 years, people were forgiven of all debts, and this made everyone joyous *(Leviticus 25:8-55)*. Forgive whatever debts *(grudges, slights, mistakes, rude words, hostility, old wounds, etc.)* you might have against every person in your family, so you may have joy in your home. How? Let grace be the theme. Forgive as the Lord has forgiven you. God allows us to choose many things, but we can not choose how and when we are born and to what family we belong. You were born into your family at a certain time and place for a reason. God has a plan for your

16

life and wants you to fulfill that plan by being all that you can be. You need the support of your family to fulfill that plan. If you are not fortunate to have parents or they are inaccessible because they reside in a different town, surround yourself with "adopted parents." When I went out-of-town to college, I found "adopted parents" in a local church: mentors whom I could look up to, ask advice from, have a Sunday lunch, or just visit. Find parental figures from whom you can relate and learn.

Sweet revenge is ironically peculiar. I challenged my parents at every avenue and tested every boundary they established. Presently, my daughter is doing the same things to me, and I must say, it is not easy. Since before she was born, we had been praying for her and getting prepared because what comes around goes around. Be nice to your parents because how you treat them might be how your children treat you!

When we deal with our family, attitude is everything. Joseph's brothers were mean to him, but God had a purpose in it because God was preparing him to be a great ruler and king *(Genesis 45:8)*. It was not fun going through the slavery, adversity, beatings or the rejection his brothers put him through. However, when the opportunity arose to pay back his brothers for the wrongs done to him, Joseph held no grudges. He found sometimes things happen for a reason. His attitude turned a bad situation into a good one. What attitude do you have with your family? Do you have a "chip" on your shoulder with them, or do you help transform bad situations into good ones?

How do we make our lives full by dividing our family? Pour yourself into each individual of your family. Investigate and evaluate their likes and dislikes. Create, sustain and maintain those relationships. Do not just look at the family as a whole, but each as an individual.

In class one day, I entered to a heated discussion with a girl yelling her father was a liar. "I just don't know what I did to make him hate me!" she blurted out. I felt sorry for the girl and wondered what on earth could have happened? "Melanie, is everything ok?" I asked as the class fell silent. "Yes," she said. Tommy, the guy sitting next to her, was

17

listening intently. "My dad won't buy me a new car." "What?" I asked. She replied, "I got into a wreck last weekend, and now, I don't have any transportation. My dad won't buy me a new car!" As I stared at her in disbelief, she continued, "It's just that…" but Tommy's words interrupted and silenced her. "At least you have a dad." We both looked at him. "My mom died when I was 8 and my dad died when I was 12. Maybe you should be happy you have a dad, instead of being mad at him for not buying you something you want, not need." Three years passed. I saw Melanie one day at a restaurant. She was home for spring break from college. As we talked, I recalled that day. "You were pretty mad that your dad wouldn't buy you a car!" I jokingly remembered. She responded, "You know, that day, my perspective on life changed because of what Tommy said. I decided to stop being a selfish jerk and hating my dad. I decided to love him and be glad for the time I have with him." Celebrate your family. Who knows when something tragic may happen and you will not have them. Tommy knows, and so does Melanie… now.

Divide your finances… John Wesley, the founder of the Methodist Movement, said, *"Earn all you can, save all you can; give all you can."* Money matters. We often vote with our money by where we choose to spend it. By our tithe, we show our dependence on God. With the products we buy, we tell the companies we like their products. When we invest in a stock, we are displaying confidence the company is going to make us money. How we spend our money is important. Learn to divide your finances by splitting your spending areas into manageable accounts. This way, you may be able to effectively trace, handle and use your money wisely.

Earn all you can… Financially, most students will not begin where their parents left off. It usually takes years of building and living. As you consider your future vocation, realistically consider how much you will make, and see if you can live within those means. If you graduate with an overwhelming debt, will you be able to make ends meet on a starting salary? While retirement may seem far in the future, start saving. Compound interest over the course of your life will earn more money for the dollar. While money is important, do not let money solely influence your vocation. I have a friend who wanted the prestige and income of a medical doctor, but he hates medicine. He is currently practicing medicine, but is not making as much as he thought. He hates his career and daily tasks, but already has too much invested to change careers. Make sure you are happy with your vocation, because if you are not enjoying your life, all the money in the world will not make you any happier.

When I was in college, I had three jobs. I worked as a waitress at the *Old Spaghetti Factory* on weeknights, as a tutor in English weekdays and at *Disneyland* on weekends. After rent and utility bills, I had very little left over for food, much less entertainment. I hardly ever had more than a dollar. I loved Diet Cokes and Snickers but did not want to spend the extra $.50. I loved *In and Out* burgers, but could only afford it once a week. I lived on water from the faucet, mustard greens and Roman Noodles, but I made it. I made my rent payment, car payment, utility bills and I did not starve. I did not have a lot (there was nothing in the front room of our apartment but an old couch and a TV tray with my Grandmother's old TV on it), but I made it work. My last year in California, I taught high school, and I was salaried. I thought I made so much money—exactly $1,200 more a month than I did when I was working the other three jobs! The weirdest thing was I still just barely made it! I made my car payment, rent and utility bills and barely had enough left over for food, much less entertainment! While the only difference in my diet was that I got *In and Out* burgers twice a week, I still only had enough for Roman Noodles and mustard greens because now I was paying my school loans, insurance and retirement! I had enough for an occasional Diet Coke out of the machine, but never had that little extra for the Snickers, and the only addition to my

apartment's front room was a new remote for the old TV! So, it did not matter if I was making a lot or a little because the money was spent. I still made it work.

Save all you can… Learn how to live on little. Whether you are a student living on little, or have a great job and earn a lot, learn to not spend your whole paycheck. Try to live on a percentage of what you make, and save some of it. In today's world, with a plethora of credit cards and loans available, many students live well beyond their means. Some students eventually pay much of their income to interest because of high debt, and therefore, feel they have no options. Ignorance is much more expensive than an education. Student loans make school accessible to some who might not have the opportunity to further their educations. Realistically keep track of what eventual payments will be so you can successfully pay back your student loans. That way, instead of paying money to interest, you can have your money work for you by allowing you more disposable income. Learn to penny-pinch on the small stuff, but splurge on the big stuff. Create a nest egg for those "just in case" times to help you out of a financial crunch. On the flip side, do not forget to live life. A couple, instead of living life, paid all their money to get out of debt. When the time came to truly live the life they had dreamed, his wife died of cancer. He regretted they never got to experience the dreams they had together because they were overly fiscally responsible.

Laura was Hispanic. She was very proud of her culture. She was also proud she was graduating with an 82 average, the top thirty percent of the class. She was going to be the first person from her family—both mother's and father's—to graduate from high school. She wanted to be the first to graduate from college, too. The problem was not getting accepted, but affording it. Because her parents were in the process of getting their American citizenship (which they had begun ten years ago and had never finished), she did not qualify for much federal aid. So, Laura took out loans. She never lived beyond the means from which she was

20

raised. She decided to attend the local community college and live at home so she could save money, but she would still be able to graduate from college and fulfill her dream—and her family's dream. "I just didn't have any choice but to take out the loans," she explained to me one day when she visited the high school. "No, Laura, the choice to take out loans is what is giving you choices for the future."

A roommate of mine in college was the worst money manager I have ever known. She got herself into a heap of trouble financially, and her poor choices are still affecting her family today. Rebekah was so happy to get out on her own. She felt like she had been given keys to her freedom when she came to college, yet she was always asking her parents for money because it went so quickly. She would get a new shirt there, a book here, dinner with a friend there, and Starbuck's coffee everyday. She hated getting in fights with her parents about money, but that is what usually happened. I would have to leave the room because the yelling was so loud—not from Rebekah, but from her mother (on the other end of the phone)! Rebekah came from the mailroom ecstatic one day. She was so bubbly and going on and on about how her money problems would all be fixed. She had received a letter "inviting" her to get a Visa card. She got one, and her credit line of $3,000 was quickly reached. I had never seen so many shoes, purses and amenities for her computer. She went on vacation to Northern California with her boyfriend, and she flew out to Texas to see her best friend. At the time, I was jealous! I wanted to do those fun things and not have to worry about money! But there was just something about the "have fun now, pay for it later" motto of credit cards I could not get over. When her Visa card had reached its limit, she got a MasterCard. Then, a Discover card. Then, an American Express card. I could not believe her. Each of the credit cards were maxed out—over thousands of dollars she owed. All this happened within six months of school—not even a whole year! Today, over 14 years later, she and her husband

21

are still trying to pay off her frivolous spending. A lot of things she wants to do in her life she is not able, just because she was not smart with her money when she was 19 years old.

Give all you can... Give some of your resources by sharing and investing in a good cause. Help another person in need. Support your local church in big and little ways. Money is a tool, and can sometimes be used for evil or good. Use your money for good. *Malachi 3:10* says to test God in this, as we will receive blessings beyond belief if we will trust Him with our finances by giving to God first. Paul shared this giving principle as he quoted Jesus saying, "It is more blessed to give than to receive" *(Acts 20:35).* Our finances can be a good indication of our spiritual life. Where and how we choose to give, spend and share, reflects on where our hearts truly are *(Luke 12:34).* The old saying, "Put your money where your mouth is" should be, "Put your money where your *heart* is."

Ken was a graduate student, with a wife and two kids, and very little income. Once, he was called to my church to preach. The church gave him a love offering of $150. I was glad for him because I knew his family could use the money. After the event, I asked him, "Ken, what did you do with the love offering? Did you take your wife out to a fancy dinner at McDonald's?" Ken laughed. "No, I thought the Lord gave me the money and I should give it to someone who needed it more than I. So, I went to the Registrar and asked to put the money towards someone's account I knew was overdrawn." I could not believe it. He took the money I thought he needed and gave it to someone he thought was more in need.

The school for which I work raises money for all sorts of things. Early in the year, we partake in collecting food for needy families. As we collected a lot of money in each class, one class brought 650 lbs. of food! Two months later, the same class adopted a foster child, Julia, 8 years old, and my students donated gifts for her. I was amazed at how much 22

students could and would raise. As a teacher, my budget for giving was spent, as I am sure were the students'. But then, one night, a tragedy occurred. A student's house burned down, along with all her belongings. The next day, the administration asked for the students to pitch in and help, and by lunchtime, the high school had raised over $2000 for her. I was amazed at my students' generosity. They had already given so much, but chose to continue to give.

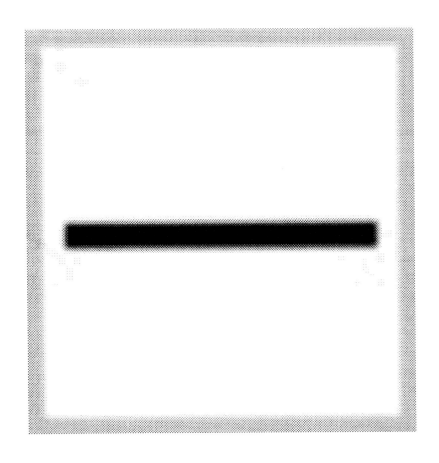

Through these he has given us his very great and precious promises, so that through them you may participate in the divine nature and escape the corruption in the world caused by evil desires.   *2 Peter 1:4*

SUBTRACT... By trusting.

Subtraction is a principle that will help you escape some of the "unpleasanties" and pitfalls of life. Experience has convinced me while moderation and temperance in all things is both commendable and beneficial, sometimes abstinence or indulgence can help us better understand the complexities of life. This is where subtraction comes. When you subtract, you might abstain from something to more fully understand sacrifice, better yourself, be healthier or make you happier. Or, you might indulge in some way, as in spiritual disciplines, in order to commune with the divine. If you can learn how to avoid and subtract certain things, attitudes or issues in life, you will be well on your way to happiness.

Subtract by trusting God's promises... Trust is a belief issue. Do you believe God's promises in the Bible are for you? God promises if we will keep our eyes on Him *(Hebrews 12:1-2)*, He will take care of us, even as a refuge in times of trouble *(Nahum 1:7)*. The promises of God are numerable, contextual and meaningful for each stage of life. God can give us strength to get through anything *(Philippians 4:13)*. Everything happens for a reason. If we will trust in Him, even though it might not be apparent to us, God will work out everything for His glory *(Proverbs 3:5-6)*. God has a plan for our lives *(Jeremiah 29.11)*, and if we seek Him with all of our heart, we will find Him *(Jeremiah 29:12-13)*. These promises can sustain with depth of truth entrenched within the soul that can shine light even in the darkest of moments. Subtract despair by believing in the hope God gives. Subtract loneliness by being involved in a community of faith. Subtract guilt and grief by believing God has won the victory over sin and death. God offers eternal life to those who believe and trust Him. We can subtract negative and detrimental attitudes and behaviors by believing in the truth of God's promises, without having to experience the pain the price of wisdom charges.

Dennis House slept every day in class. If he was awake, it would be to tell a wild tale from the night before:

26

his car was totaled, he spent the night in a ditch hiding from the police, he danced wildly before some girls; it was always something he deemed entertaining. Then, he stopped sleeping and started announcing—everyday—"I'm sober, Mrs. Welshimer!" Without fail, everyday he would come in with his announcement. If he did not say it, I would ask him why. Then, he would immediately tell me again—"Still sober!" Later in the year, while we discussed this topic, he admitted the reason he had drunk so much was because he was not very good at talking to girls, which caused him to be lonely. So, to cover up his loneliness, he would drink (and drink and drink). He finally said, "It wasn't worth it. All the headaches, the stupid trouble I got into with the police and my parents—it wasn't and isn't worth it. I wish I was like some of my smarter friends who just avoid drinking and those problems altogether." I wished every one of my students could have heard him.

Subtract by experiencing God… God made you for Himself! You were created with a void in your life that can only be filled by God. In life, we try to fill this "void" with things, pleasures, education, relationships, sports, busyness and tons of other "stuff." While all this may be good or bad, it only fills the void temporarily. Long-term satisfaction and fulfillment comes when we allow God to fill that void in our lives.

You can talk about God a lot, but unless you experience Him, words are usually just words. When I tell my daughter not to touch the hot pan, I explain she will get burned if she does. Usually, she will go ahead and touch the pan anyway. It is not until she touches the pan herself and gets burned that she experiences the burning for herself. Then she will believe and trust what I have told her. Sometimes it comes to that. We hear if we touch the pan, it will burn us. We understand the principle, but we touch the pan anyway, because we do not understand the severity of the heat. When you play with fire, you may get burned. King David played with fire when he sought out Bathsheba and entertained impure and even criminal thoughts to fulfill his unholy desires *(2 Samuel 11)*. Nathan told him about it as if it happened to someone else. David became infuriated *(2 Samuel 12:4-6)*. It was not until Nathan openly rebuked David that he understood the atrocity of his actions. He experienced the real guilt that comes with horrible deeds *(2 Samuel 12)*. Experiences can change us. They make up our history, our worldview and who we are, either for good or bad.

Christ endured the cross and shed His blood so we might experience God's presence. It is that presence and real feeling of assurance that "God is with you" which can give you confidence in subtracting the things of this world that drag you down. Have a spiritual experience. Seek it out. God promises if we will try to find Him, we will *(Matthew 7:7-8)*. Find a local church. Make time to be alone. Have a quiet time with just you and your Bible. Journal. Do not just be a religious person on the outside who knows all about God but has not truly experienced Him. Ask God for insight *(James 1:5)*. Reading the Bible for five minutes with an open heart to God can do more good than fifty hours studying the Scriptures with a critical eye. Be open and ready, because once you taste the divine, you will want more and more of God. That desire for Him will help subtract some of the implosive behavior and attitudes that can could derail your happiness and success.

Heidi was a wild one. She often came to class with different colored hair and unusual outfits. I doubt she owned a pair of shoes that were not three-inch high heels, and to say she spent a little time on her make-up would be an understatement. But it was not her outside appearance that caused me to say she was wild. It was her stories, the things I heard from the administration and the things I saw on the news that caused me to say she was a wild one. She shared her story with me. I thought it was very inspirational. She was driving her car—in an intoxicated state, due to drugs, not alcohol. She was driving her car faster than she should have been—90 in a 30 mph zone. She raced by her mother's work and saw her mother's car. A scene instantly flashed through her mind and shook her. The scene was her best friend's mom crying at her best friend's funeral (who had been killed

28

in a boating accident six months earlier). **She saw her mom's car and did not want her mom to have to go through that same thing.** She somehow got a picture of herself and how she was acting, and she was flabbergasted. **Heidi was appalled at the way she was living her life and wanted to change it.** "As I experienced God in that moment, I saw Him crying at His Son's funeral," she explained. "And I thought, what am I doing with my life?" In that moment she decided to change her habits. **Heidi still wears unusual things, and still does her hair in different colors every other week, but you can sense she is not the same. She was a changed person because of that experience.**

      <u>Subtract by praying</u>... Are you anxious? Pray about it *(Philippians 4:6)*. Having problems with your roommate? Pray for him/her *(Matthew 5:44)*. Unsure about your future? Pray for guidance *(Proverbs 16:3)*. Worried about your family, friends, grades or problems? Often, we bear the burden in our lives that God wants to bear for us. He can not, until we give them to Him. Prayer is not only for you, but also for God. Talk to Him. Tell God what is on your mind. Listen. Absorb. We can subtract worry, fear and frustration by lifting our concerns and fully surrendering to God in prayer.

      Charlie Rhodes had some horrible things happen to him. When he was 12, his parents, who had been abusive and addicted to drugs, tried to sell him and his little sisters to get drugs. They were shipped off to several different houses by Child Protective Services. When he turned 18, he tried to get custody of his sisters to keep his family together, but he was caught at a party where among the beverages, there was alcohol. Though he himself was not drinking, he was taken to jail for the night anyway. Now the courts are not looking at him as a favorable guardian for his younger sisters because of a police record. He feels cheated and alone. I felt sorry for him but had no idea what I could do as he told me this story. I just looked at him, knowing he was not a religious young man and offered him the only kind of help I

29

thought I could. "I am praying for you Charlie." He was moved. "Thanks, Mrs. Welshimer! I need all the prayer I can get!" I think he was genuinely glad I was going to pray for him.

One day a girl came in crying, who was usually all smiles. I asked if she needed to go to the bathroom. I encouraged her friend to invite her outside to talk if she wanted. But Abby did not leave; she just sat there as we carried on with class. After the assignment had been given, I sat at my desk and she asked me if I could talk to her in the hallway. She thought she was pregnant. "My best guy friend and I got a little carried away the other weekend, and it led to more than we both wanted. Now, I am scared to tell my friend that I might be pregnant. I know he will get mad at me and not want to be my friend anymore. What do I do, Mrs. Welshimer? I don't want this to hurt our friendship because he is a good friend and very important to me. I am a Christian and know that I should not have let things get this far. I am usually not like this. I have been praying that our relationship will not be changed." I explained her concern should not be only for the loss of her friend, but also for the care of a new life. "Abby, when you made the decision to go one step further with your friend—your relationship changed. Now there is more to worry and pray about than a loss of a friendship."

Subtract by perspective… Life is short, but can also seem to be long. God desires to give us both short and long-term happiness. Things might bring long-term happiness, but short-term pain. While other things bring short-term happiness, but long-term pain. Perspective helps us to decipher what is worth our time, effort and energy, both short-term and long-term.

One Thursday night, you might be asked to go watch a ball game with your buddies instead of studying for a test the next day. Sounds like a no-brainer *(of course you'd go to the game and then stay up all night studying)*, but this can be more complicated than it may sound. Spending time with friends and building meaningful relationships is a very important long-term goal, but so is school. Learn what you need to do. Decipher between the things you *want* to do and the things you *have* to do.

In your struggle to get the most out of your time, experiences and life, ask yourself, "How can this help me?" *(1 Corinthians 6:12)*. While some things are permissible, are they beneficial? If you start it now, will you still master it in one year, or will it become your master? Is this quest I am about to embark going to feed my spiritual side or my carnal side? *(Galatians 6:7-8)*. Is there a long-term benefit in it for me, or is the pleasure a fleeting moment? Are there negative side effects to this fleeting moment? What will it cost me in the long run?

While teaching at Baylor, I was cornered by a student who had not been in class for a week. He was trying to turn in a paper that was due two days ago. He tried to offer me an explanation. "I have been ministering. I know that God wants me to be a minister. I have been spending evenings going to homeless shelters and talking and praying with people. It has been amazing, and every time I go I am convinced all the more this is why I am here—to minister to the people of Waco. I have not been to class lately because I stay out so late ministering. This is why my paper is late. I had a big event to attend over the weekend and did not get a chance to finish it until now." He handed me the paper— proud of himself for explaining his calling, glad that I was a professed "Christian" and could understand. "Stan, do you know why you are here?" "Yeah, like I said, to minister." "No, God brought you here to study. He may very well be calling you to be a minister, and that is a really great and wonderful thing, but He called you to Baylor to be a student. And if you are not careful to go to class, turn your papers in on time and maintain your grades, you will fail. Then you will not be here next semester in order to minister." He never missed another class.

My school has a very strict hair code. Joey did not want to cut his hair. It was early April when the

administration first approached him about getting a haircut. Joey instantly refused. They gave him several warnings and then placed him in ISS. Joey still refused. They even told him he could not participate in the graduation ceremonies if he did not get his hair cut. Joey's mom called me. "Is there anything that you can do to convince my son to get a haircut? You see, he will be the first person in our family to graduate from high school. My parents, in-laws and cousins were all planning on attending his graduation. They already bought plane tickets and made hotel reservations. We were going to throw a big party for him. I can't talk any sense into him... can you?" I felt sorry for Joey's mom. As I talked to Joey, he said he was "punishing" the administration for how it had treated all the guys who wanted long hair, by choosing not to get his hair cut. What he did not realize was the ones he was really "punishing" were his parents, grandparents and other family members who were excited to see the first of their family graduate (the ones who had already paid their hard earned money for plane tickets). Joey did not care. He still refused to cut his hair. And he, nor anyone else in his family, participated at graduation.

Subtract by being yourself... Americans are the best at acting. We can put on a face for any occasion. The *"corporate syndrome"* is a condition of the personality that happens when we keep everyone at arm's length and do not risk being ourselves, for fear of retribution or rejection. If you are going to have friends, real friends, risk being vulnerable and open by being yourself. God made you wonderfully in His image *(Genesis 1:27)*, and made you exactly the way He wants you, warts and all. Be yourself. Subtract the exhausting exercise of being insincere, fake and phony, and enjoy whom you are and what you like to do.

A major reason some are reluctant to open up is many people do not like themselves. Individuals fear if other people saw her/his real personality then she/he would be instantly rejected and excluded. What a sad way to go through life. Work on liking yourself and enjoying who you are. One of the assumptions when Jesus says to "love God and others" *(Matthew 22:37-40)* is that we first love ourselves. It is often hard to love God and others if we first do not have the foundation of love for ourselves. Subtract loneliness, insecurity and self-doubt by exploring yourself, by deciding what you enjoy, with whom who you connect with and what you do not particularly care for. Sometimes, what we really feel and think is not good or nice. A person can be brutally honest and even mean, and use "that's just me" as an excuse. Work on subtracting negativity, and when you do not have anything nice to say or good to contribute, do not say anything at all. The old saying "Sticks and stones may hurt my bones, but words will never hurt me" is not true! Bones and bruises will often heal quickly, but wounds of the heart and soul can last a lifetime, and those destructive wounds usually come from our mouths *(Proverbs 12:25, 15:1)*. Be yourself, but when in doubt, be nice!

At Baylor, I taught Writing and Research. I was 22 when I first started teaching there and I wanted the students—some of whom were older than I—to take me seriously. On the first day of class, I wore a black power suit. I came into the room, appearing more confident than I felt, and I went through the syllabus. My speech began like this: "My name is MISS Price (I was not yet married and this was my maiden name). It's not MS. Price because I am not anyone's mistress, and it is not MRS. Price because I am not married. It's MISS Price, and I expect you all to get it right." Then, I began a diatribe about my class. When I was done, I walked out without offering anyone a chance to talk to me. I always had two or three people drop the class after that first day! However, by the end of the semester, when my students actually got to know me, they were always vocal about the misconception they had of me that first day. They said they went home scared of me and the requirements of the course. Once they got to know me, though, and realized my personality did not coincide with the person who entered the room on that first day of class, they were all relieved— and happy they got to know the real me.

Courting, dating, engagement and marriage can seem like a "bait & switch" process. During the courting stages, we try and impress the other person. While dating, we put our best foot forward for hours at a time as we get all dolled up for the other person. In engagement, we usually are just so thrilled we have a soul-mate we agree to almost anything for the sake of the relationship. Then, the marriage comes. I will never forget the awkward moments of the first time my wife heard me snore, smelled my morning dragon-breath or started realizing my peculiar quirks. While I am not saying to bear your soul and expose all of your inflictions on the first date, you can minimize those awkward moments in life by subtracting imitation with authenticity. Sooner or later, your true self will be exposed for what it is and who you truly are.

Third period two students were discussing their futures. If both of the students were not married by the time they were 30, they would marry each other. They asked me what I thought. I looked from the tall dark headed beauty to the short, light-headed guy. "I'll tell you, Adam, you sure would be lucky to get a girl like Kristie." He immediately went on the defense. "She will be lucky to have me! Whoever I end up with will be lucky to get a good looking, respectful guy like me!" I shook my head. "Adam, you got the idea all wrong. You know you will have met 'the one' when you think, 'why is this great girl with me?'" Kristie smiled. "And the girl will think the same thing of you." Adam just shook his head. "That's why I don't think a marriage between the two of you will ever work. You both need to be head over heels in love with each other, thinking that the other is the best thing that has ever happened to you. That's love."

Subtract by guarding your heart... "Above all else, guard your heart, for it is the wellspring of life" *(Proverbs 4:23).* God is all about "the heart" as He does not consider outward appearances, but the attitude of the heart *(1 Samuel 16:7).* Isaiah prophesies about the coming Christ when Jesus is described as having no outward appearances people would desire, but people would be spiritually attracted to His heart *(Isaiah 53:2)*. Paul says God does not judge by external appearances *(Galatians 2:6)*, but people can come to salvation by believing in their hearts *(Romans 10:9-10)*. How we feel and what we hold in our hearts matters to God. While you can not "judge a book by it's cover," your heart is a sacred and fine pearl. You need to be careful who gets permission and access to that pearl. Be wise by guarding your heart and not giving it to dogs or pigs, so that they can trample on it *(Matthew 7:6)*. Save and give your heart to things and people that will not hurt you but make you better.

Relationships and love: they are topics most students, especially girls, take seriously. Shawna was a beautiful, popular girl who had been dating the same guy, who appeared to be her polar opposite, for two and a half years. I knew something was wrong when she came into class one day with a tear stained face. She put her head on her desk and did not lift it the rest of class. That afternoon, I received an email from her mother that explained Shawna's boyfriend had broken up with her. Her heart was broken. She came to see me before school the next day. "People keep telling me that they can't believe we were together in the first place. They think just because he may not look like someone I would want to date that we could've been together. That's not true. We may have been different on the outside, but we really are the same! We both love the same things and we had plenty to talk about all the time! We have the same values and hold the same things true. That's why this hurts so much. I feel like I have broken up with my best friend, and everyone is happy about it." She was hurt about the break up, but even more upset about the "talk" that was going around school. "I wish people wouldn't judge me by my appearance, but get to know me, and him, then maybe they could understand what I am going through."

God desires inward virtues not outward vessels. The Bible is full of "good" people that did great things outwardly, but were still far from the saving grace of God because their hearts were cold. There are also wonderful stories about how God used outwardly "bad" people to do His work and be His people. The Pharisees were "good" people on the outside, but their hearts were cold to God. There is an old saying: "I don't drink, smoke, or chew, and I don't go with girls who do" which can be a creed for many Christian students. While this rule of thumb may keep you out of trouble, it is still just a mark of the outward life. A person might not do those things, but still might have a lost soul. I have known many good Christians who struggle with these issues, and yet I have also known some reprehensible villains who would not touch the stuff. While usually the attitudes of our hearts indicate our outward actions and words, just saying the right words or doing the right things on the outside, while virtuous, is not God's desire. God's desire is our hearts being right with Him *(Mark 7:6)*. It is what comes out of a person that makes him or her clean or unclean *(Mark 7:20)*. Our outward actions and inward hearts should be aligned with God so our desires may be fully satisfied *(Psalm 37:4)*. The kingdom of God is not just about the outside, but also about the inward virtues of truth *(Romans 14:17)*. Do not only strive to attain outward virtues, but also aspire for the unseen virtues God desires.

He was going to college on a football scholarship. He was voted class favorite. He was good looking. Though most students might get in trouble for some of the things he was involved in—he never did. He was blessed—and he let everyone around him know it. We were choosing research topics in a first come, first serve fashion at 7:00 am. I came in around 6:45. I set up my "station" to be ready for the maul of students that would show up early. In walked Joey. I looked at the clock—6:50. I wondered how in the world he got into the school? The principal was not even supposed to open the door until 7:00—which, with travel time, the students should not be showing up until 7:04 or so. "The Beatles." He said. "What?" I looked up at him perplexed. "I want the Beatles." Wow. He somehow managed to get

into the school a different way than the rest of the students, whereas I had seen a group of students waiting outside. Where did he fit into that line? "Joey, I am sorry but I am not going to start signing people up until 7:00." He stared at me and started to laugh, like I was joking. Where was his integrity? What made him better than my other students? The fact that he was charming? "I am sorry; you need to go wait with the other students." He was mad to say the least, but Conrad, who had been in line since 5:30 that morning for the same topic would have been more upset. I was surprised that someone who was so "great" on the outside had so little integrity on the inside.

Danny was all smiles. He was sweet. He always knew the right thing to say to get himself out of a bad situation. We had the rough draft of our big research paper due. The night before, my family and I went to a school basketball game. We sat on the second tier of the stadium. A loud ruckus came from the student section of the building. We looked over and I saw Danny there, with his friends; they had just broken a chair. They were laughing. A principal came over and skirted them away. After we left the game, we went out for ice cream. We left about 9:30 (I remember being worried about getting the kids to bed). As we left, Danny and his group of friends drove up—guess we had a good idea! The next day, I picked up papers just as I had every year. Third period came around. Danny came in—sad and distraught. "Oh Mrs. Welshimer," he started. "I worked on the research paper last night from the moment I got home from work. Then, at 8:00, my sister called, as I was working on my paper! I had to go pick her up in Austin because her car had died and she had no way back! Please give me one more day and I will have it done!" I stared into his pleading, burdensome, lying eyes. I could not believe he was staring me in the eye and lying through his teeth. "Danny, you can turn it in tomorrow." He smiled gleefully. "Oh, I just have two questions." His prideful look changed with my words. "First, did you get in trouble for breaking the chair? And what kind of ice cream did you get?" Trust is not built on smiles and sweet words, but on inward virtue.

Have you ever been there but not really been there, when you do something, but your heart really is not in it, so you just go through the motions? Many times we are physically there, but get preoccupied with the fascination of outward things like sports, alcohol, education, work, family, finances, retirement or TV. We daydream about them as we zone out. While sometimes these fascinations can be good or bad, they usually are just outward and temporal and are in contention for our souls. Wherever you are, whatever you are doing, be there. Do not disengage by daydreaming or thinking about something else. When you work, work at it with all of your heart, as for the Lord *(Colossians 3:23)*. When you are at church, worship with all of your heart. Do not just attend in body, but also in spirit.

After we turn in research papers, we watch a movie of a book we read. It lasts six days. The students are excited to actually get to watch something that long. During this time, we have writing conferences, in which we discuss the students' documentation in their research papers. This information is on their calendars, and on the board, not to mention we are actually watching the movie as I am calling students up to my desk during it. Every day I have a movie countdown. "We have four more movie days!" "We have three more movie days!" This is very annoying to me... I can not imagine how annoying it must be for the students! This one guy who had *not* missed class all semester came into my fourth period. "What are we doing today? Watching a movie? Writing conferences, what is that?" I did not even respond. One of my favorite girls did for me. "She only says it about seven times every class period. Where have you been?" Even if one does not enjoy class, you have to go, so you might as well be present, in body and in spirit for it. He not only annoyed me, but he looked silly in front of his friends as well.

Subtract regrets… Many people go through life full of regret: "Woulda, shoulda, coulda." They beat themselves up over their failure to either have the backbone to say "no" or the courage to rise to the occasion. Some things in life you may not be good at, but do not let that stop you from trying or living. Try to subtract regrets by asking yourself beforehand, "What would it hurt if I do this?" "Will this glorify God?" *(1 Corinthians 10:31)*. "If my family, friends or church knew about this, would they be honored or ashamed?" "Does this fit into God's plan for my life?" If, in your contemplation, you can answer these questions with true conviction and honesty, then be fully engaged in what you are doing. Try it. Live it. Make the most of every opportunity *(Colossians 4:5)*, especially in the things of faith. One of the biggest regrets I have in life is I did not take a stronger stand for God in relationships growing up. I could have loved more, met more people, done more for God and told more people about the Good News of the Gospel. Do not let that happen to you. Ask, seek, and find *(Luke 11:9-10)*, and do not be afraid to try new possibilities in life, education, relationships and faith. Then, hopefully, many years from now, when you look back upon your life, you can cherish the memories and join Paul in saying "I have fought the good fight, I have finished the race" *(2 Timothy 4:7)*, or in my words, humbly proclaim, "What a ride!"

Maybe you already have some regret of things you did or did not do. In the dark nights of the soul, look for the touch of God. God sent Christ to relieve you of your burdens *(Matthew 11:28)* and free you *(John 8:36)* for joyful living. Give those regrets to God *(Philippians 4:6)*, as you let the old go and enjoy being the beautiful new creation He has created you to be *(2 Corinthians 5:17)*.

Anton knew that smoking was bad for him, as he was a singer and an athlete. His mom had been on the school board. His sister had been the student council president her senior year. He felt like he had a lot to live up to. He smoked, and people knew, but he did not care. When the drug dogs seized Anton's car, rumors started flying. It was

not the cigarettes or the prescription medicine that got him in trouble, but some hard core drugs—and a lot of it. It turned out Anton was selling the drugs on campus. Some people did not care, others were worried about him, but most were just disappointed. How could someone with so much potential—a career in sports or music, with obvious leadership abilities—ruin his chances at life by selling drugs? His mom was devastated. His choir teacher and baseball coach were upset with him. One day, he shared this with me: "If I had only known that this was going to destroy my future and the hope people had in me, I never would have done it."

Being in class, I usually give my students plenty of time to visit. In doing so, when I want their full attention and ask them to be quiet, they usually comply. A few students and I were visiting about Corrigan—a week near Valentine's Day when the girl asks the guy out. One guy was boasting about his date and how he could not wait to spend time alone with her—"whatever happens will be good!" He laughed, supposing I did not understand his underlying meaning. "Tim," I said, "What about your girlfriend? She lives in another town, right?" Tim did not even skip a beat. "Yep! What she doesn't know can't hurt her!" His friends in the class laughed. I was sick to my stomach for his girlfriend. How could this guy do these shameful things behind her back? What would happen if he were exposed? I never before wished I had someone's phone number than at that moment.

Subtract those "one nights"… A guy named "Buck" really wanted to graduate with a blaze. The night before the last day of school, he stole the Ronald McDonald statue from McDonald's and hoisted it up on the school roof. In an instant, he became the star of the senior class of 1991. While he reveled in all of his glory and our envy, he did not graduate with the rest of the class *(even though his whole family traveled in to witness it)*. He faced criminal charges and litigation for months to come. I remember what he said as they cuffed him at school: "If you play with fire, you might get burned" *(I later found that in Proverbs 6:27)*. Subtract those "one nights" that might bring temporal fame and pleasure, but could negatively affect your future. Consider the implications, and remember that those "one nights" and parties come and go, but the consequences could be for a lifetime.

What could the harm be in a bonfire? It is one night when all the seniors get together for fun and encouragement for the Homecoming football game, a once in a lifetime thing. Party...girls...the works—only for one night, right? That is what most students think, but that one night changed Raul's life forever. He was excited about being in the middle of the bonfire. He was the one who arranged for all the wood to come. He was the one who text messaged all of his friends, and their friends, about where the true location of the bonfire would be. The night commenced. He was having a blast—well, what he could remember of it anyway. He had a little too much to drink and a little too much to smoke. He saw the huge mass of fire and wood in front of him. "Bet you can't jump over that mass!" his friend suggested. They all started taunting him and telling him he could or could not do so. Raul's judgment was so clouded the fire appeared smaller than it actually was. He backed his truck up to the side of the fire to have a short running start (the length of the truck bed) and started to jump. He could not, of course, get over the huge gulf of flames, as he fell into the middle of the fire. Students who were clear headed enough to understand the serious nature of the situation rushed to get him out. He survived, but he was paralyzed from the waist down, and his face was charred beyond recognition. That is all it took to change Raul's life, present and future. One night. One bad decision.

<u>**Subtract those "moments"**</u>**...** There was a senior who was the "all-star" kid who had a bright future. He was the star quarterback of the football team, valedictorian, youth group leader and student council president. Everyone in his small town

knew and loved him. He had a girlfriend for two years whom he was sure he would eventually marry. Well, she broke up with him in a publicly humiliating way. He was distraught and took it really hard. The next Friday he was driving around in his car with the music blaring, sulking his wounds. As he drove by his ex's house, he saw his best friend's car in the driveway. He was infuriated, and in a moment of shear rage, pulled out a knife and started slitting the tires of his friend's car. The loud pop of the tires drew his best friend out of his ex's house. The "all-star" transformed into an "animal" as he turned around and unleashed his fury by stabbing his friend. Once he realized what he had done, he regretted it immediately, but could do nothing but call for help. His friend ended up dying, and this "all-star" ended up in prison as he watched his dreams evaporate, all because of one moment! **All it takes is one bad moment to ruin a lifetime of good moments.** Minimize "bad moments" in your life. Many people in prison wish they could take back just one moment, but have to pay for that moment with the rest of their lives. Be on your guard because the enemy is looking for someone to devour, and once you give him an inch, he will do everything in his power to destroy you *(1 Peter 5:8).*

   Keep watch because you do not know when your time will pass *(Matthew 24:42).* You are not invincible. All will die and everything has to come to an end. Early in my ministry, a student died in a horrible accident. Although that person came to church regularly, I was not sure where he stood in his faith. Ever since then, I make it my goal to prepare students for the afterlife by sharing the Gospel with them *(John 3:16),* and encouraging them to live as those prepared to die. Sometimes this is the last thing we think about. But, God wants it to be of "first importance" *(1 Corinthians 15:1-5).* Are you ready to die? It seems when that "moment" comes, there is peace for you and your loved ones if you have answered the question, "What will you do with Jesus?" Many times we get so distracted we forget what is really important. **Subtract distractions in your life by listening** to God's voice in your heart *(John 10:27).* Do not wait until it is too late, but seek to subtract "negative moments" by having "spiritual moments" and hearing God's voice in your heart.

I had a student who hated school. He was always getting into trouble but he wanted his diploma, so he was trying to stick it out until graduation. One day, Shane was "minding his own business" when the principal told him he needed to shave. Shane said he was going to hit this principal the next time he came up to him. "What do you think?" he asked me. "Shane, if you hit him, you can get into a lot of trouble, not to mention that he can sue you because you are eighteen, and you might jeopardize your graduation. You are so close Shane...just months away, and if you lose your temper for a minute, you will lose a lot more in the long run. Next time this happens, bite your tongue, hold your fists together, and walk away. Don't get into trouble before graduation." Shane controlled himself and graduated with his class. A little short-term self-control helped Shane in the long run. Consider your goals and the long-term consequences before you act.

Subtract by taming your emotions... The difference between an amateur and a professional is the professional will rise to the occasion, even when he/she does not feel like it. The reason Michael Jordan was so good at basketball is because he was committed to practice, especially when he did not feel like practicing. Feelings can either help us or hurt us. Our feelings can betray us, so we do not need to fully trust in them. Some days, I do not feel like being a minister, a parent, a husband or even a Christian, but I have made those commitments beforehand. So when those feelings arise, my faith and commitment can help me tame my emotions. Emotions can be very strong and convincing, especially if we have not already made a commitment. I encourage students to decide to let "true love wait" before experiencing any negative consequences. **What makes humanity different than any other species in the animal kingdom is our ability to reason and our capacity for self-control.** That is why the dog goes through the trash even after you tell him not to a hundred times. You were created with a mind and a particular self will to make the right choices. Use it. Jesus came to take away our sins, not our minds. So think before you act. Remember you can always say no. Weigh your choices carefully because God promises He is faithful and will always provide a way out for you *(1 Corinthians 10:13).*

Learn to tame your emotions by controlling your thoughts. Subtract destruction by taking your thoughts captive *(2 Corinthians 10:5).* Subtract sadness by remembering the times you were happy. Subtract stress by remembering times of idle boredom. Subtract failure with the memory of past successes. Subtract hesitancy with action. Sometimes failure is not our downfall, but success can puff us up to new levels of defeat. When you feel invincible, try to control the weather. When you experience moments of greatness, think of who you were before you had it, and how you got there. When you overindulge, remember the children who are starving in the world. When you feel powerful, consider the infinite galaxy. In doing so, neither riches nor poverty, prosperity nor adversity, complements nor complaints, fame nor shame, friend nor foe, will be able to sway you from the confidence you have in the person God has created you to be. Then, you will be able to withstand anything that comes your way.

Jake, Ryan and Jeff are guys who, at the beginning of the year, had it all together. They came to class on time. They may not have made perfect grades, but they were always engaged in the work. They would think about stories over the night and come in asking philosophical questions the next day. It would drive me nuts! I felt like I was teaching a college class, but it was encouraging they were allowing the ideas and concepts of what I was teaching to influence their thoughts. Then, in a month's time, one by one, they all turned 18. The three guys started being late to class—a lot. They were stuck in the tardy room most of the time, and ended up having detention and Saturday school as a result. When they did make it to class on time, they were usually

asleep. I was worried about them, as they used to be so alert. What happened? "What is the deal with Jake, Ryan and Jeff?" I asked the class one day. "They are all 18 now," I was informed by one of my students. I was confused. "So?" "They are going to the strip clubs every night." Oh! Jake finally made it to class one day. "You spend all night carousing so you can't come to school the next day?" I inquired as he laughed. "It's weird Mrs. Welshimer; at first I went just because everyone else did. It was fun—the thing to do. But now I can't get enough of it. I think about it; I dream about it; like I said, I just can't get enough of it. I really wish it did not control my thoughts as much as it does." I had a great solution: "So don't go anymore." Sounded pretty simple to me. "I can't though; it's like a drug. The more I get, the more I want," he confessed.

Sometimes students are in a bad mood because they do not agree with the school's rules. The guys want to be able to wear their hair long. The girls want to be able to wear their nose rings or jeans with holes in them. One day the students were discussing the dress code in class. "It was a frayed edge on the bottom of my jeans. It's not like my shirt said something inappropriate or was too tight. They make me so mad." Mary was complaining. It would have been easy to agree with her there was no harm in wearing a pair of jeans with a frayed edge. I could have said a lot of things, but that would not have been professional. Whether we agree or disagree with the rules of the school, we belong to the school, and therefore must adhere to the rules. I need to support the school and the administration that overall supports me. So, I responded in the way I thought was appropriate. "Mary, I am sorry you had to change your pants, but the rules of the school are you can't wear frayed pants."

<u>**Subtract by taming the tongue**</u>... The tongue can be a powerful tool. Many people are addicted to all kinds of things that have to do with their tongues. The tongue can help or hurt,

45

as what we say can either bless or curse *(James 3:2-12)*. The tongue is a mystical thing. It can reveal our inmost thoughts, deepest feelings and true heart's wants and desires *(Matthew 12:34-36)*. What we say is powerful. It can devastate a child's self esteem, acquit an innocent man, ruin a career or bring salvation to a lost soul *(Romans 10:13)*. It is not an easy task to learn how to tame the powerful use of the tongue because what we say is always in the present. Do you ever seem to beat yourself up because you should have said something you did not, or should not have said something you did? It is like a can of shaving cream: once you press the button and the shaving cream comes out, there is no way to put it back in the can. The past is done. What is said is said, and even the most undeveloped person can come up with something to say, after the fact. Because the future is so uncertain, we often have no idea what to say because we do not know what we are dealing with. The challenge is to tame what you say in the present.

To tame your tongue and stay out of trouble, **grow up.** When you were a child, everyone laughed at cute cut-ups, but now is the time to start acting, thinking and talking like an adult in adult ways *(1 Corinthians 13:11)*. One of the great comedian Chris Farley's downfalls is he could not put away the things of his youth and "grow up" into adulthood. Many guys in college are so insecure with themselves and intimidated by collegiate women they must have a drink in their hands to medicate and give security before engaging in conversation with the opposite sex. They do not understand that with a drink in their hands they do not look much cooler. It is time to grow up by putting the things of children away and start acting like adults.

Brian Cower challenged me every day in one way or another. His behavior was an eye-opener and his attitude was laced with constant negativity. More times than not, I just let him do whatever he needed to get through the day— lay on the floor to read, work on his Economics homework, or sleep. I was so happy when he was absent. One day the students were turning in an assignment, which we had been working on in class all week. Brian came up to turn in his

assignment. He had only completed part of it. "Where is the rest of it?" I asked. "What?" I explained he was missing a part of the paper. All of a sudden he was so angry he threw the book he was holding across the room. Everyone gasped, as they were hesitant to see how I would react to his outburst. I calmly looked at him and asked him to leave the room. Once outside, instead of chastising him, I asked him if he wanted to go to the library to complete the assignment. He agreed. When he came back, he was apologetic, not only to me, but also to the entire class. "Thanks for not overreacting to my overreaction," he said. I had surprised him by reacting to his outburst in an unexpected way. After that, he was still a challenge, but his attitude carried a positive tone.

While we often talk without thinking or listening, God challenges us to be **slow to speak, quick to listen and slow to become angry** *(James 1:19)*. Be slow to speak. Do not say the first thing that comes to your mind. In conversations, learn what the real issues are so you may fully address the situation with your words. Take time to observe before you speak, and consider the different options you have. When you speak, do not let it be unwholesome or hurtful. Let your words build others up, so those who hear them might benefit from your words *(Ephesians 4:29)*. Who wants to be around people who constantly complain, bicker, cut-down and hurt others? While words like this can be entertaining at times on TV, in real life, negative words are like a cancer that destroys as it spreads. Let your conversation be full of grace *(Colossians 4:6)*, compassion and understanding. When you do, you speak as God's spokesperson *(2 Corinthians 5:20)*. Carefully choose your words. For by your words you can be acquitted, and by your words you can be condemned *(Matthew 12:37)*. In our world of instant email, text messages and letters, the vessels of communication can be dangerous and even proof of criminal activity if taken in the wrong context. So, be wise in your words. Be quick to listen. Carefully examine what is being said. Sometimes, you can see what is being said without listening to words. Body demeanor can tell a lot, with communication being

70% non-verbal. Often, what is being said is not really what is meant. I once got chewed out by a person for some mundane detail. In the course of our conversation, I learned the source of his anger was not me or the issue, but something else. I asked him three times, "Is this really the issue that's bothering you?" Finally, after beating around the bush, he confessed the real issue was not what we were talking about but something deeper. Then we could address this deeper issue, but it came only because I listened to his heart, not his words. Find out what is really being said, not just in words, but by listening.

Be slow to become angry. Many a relationship, job and life are ruined by words said in anger and revenge. Do not say words in haste, anger or revenge, but leave room for God's wrath and grace in your life and your words *(Romans 12:19)*. During the darkest moments in the life of Abraham Lincoln, when people were saying personal things against him, he never publicly struck back. Instead, he would write strongly worded letters, personally gloat over them for a short while, and then burn them. It is when you do not say anything at all that you might be considered wise *(Proverbs 17:28)*. When a couple breaks up and continually fights, they at least give the other person the time and energy of the fight, thus showing some feelings toward the other person. It is when the other person totally disengages, does not care who gets the blame and does not care what the other person thinks when the relationship is really over. Control malicious words by taming your tongue. Be slow to speak, quick to listen and slow to become angry.

Paul Ricks was a very respectful young man. He was kind, funny, interesting and always nice. His class was a bit rowdy. A group of people in the class had been friends for a long time, and though they were all very nice, they liked to talk. Paul was a member of this group. He liked to talk, but whenever I asked the class to settle down, he would be the one to help quiet the other members of the class as well. Paul came to class one day in a bad mood. He obviously had a bad day. He did not greet me or anyone else like he usually did. He went to his desk and put his head down. I knew he did

not play well in the important soccer game the previous night and he and his girlfriend were in a fight. In the middle of class, and my lecture, he turned to the girl behind him and they started whispering. "Paul, would you please be quiet?" He lashed out at me. "I am not interrupting class. I am talking quietly and what I am talking about is more important in my life than what you are talking about." I could not believe my ears. Was this the same sweet Paul that was always in my class? I was stunned by his response, and I was not sure what to do. He turned around in a huff and put his head down on his desk. I was mad, but did not want to lose my cool; I knew he had a horrible day. So, I did not do anything. I waited until the next day to address the issue. But before I had the opportunity, he approached me, "Mrs. Welshimer, I am sorry at how I responded to you in class yesterday. I had such a bad day and I was in such a bad mood that I took it out on you. Thank you for being understanding and not getting me into more trouble." I was glad I did not let my anger of the moment take over.

It was seventh period. It had been a long day and my class was loud. I had two students who started talking while they still had vocabulary quizzes on their desks. Without even giving them a warning, I jumped all over them. "Taylor and Jasmine, be quiet! You all could be considered cheating with a quiz on your desk and talking! You are lucky I don't send you to the office immediately!" The outburst was so unlike me some of the students in the back were not sure if I was serious or joking. The girls were humiliated. They turned a dark shade of red and were quickly quiet. I felt horrible. The students had not done anything all that bad. I did not even give them a warning. I was so disappointed in the way I had treated them. The bell rang and away they flew out the door. All night I felt bad. I prayed about it, told my husband, called my mom and emailed my best friend. I fretted about my anger so much I even *dreamed* about the girls and an ugly encounter. I prayed about it all night. I woke up the next day determined to make things right. I

49

promised myself I was never going to blow up or speak in anger like that again. Seventh period finally came around. I stood up as class began, "I want to apologize to Taylor and Jasmine in front of the class." They immediately were intrigued by what I had to say. "Yesterday I blew up at both of you and I shouldn't have. Though you shouldn't have been talking during the quiz, I am sorry I was rude to you by blowing up the way I did." They both nodded an agreement to my apology. One girl said, "Wow! I've never heard a teacher apologize before; that's cool." All I knew was I had a long dreadful night the evening before and never wanted to agonize about a school situation at home again. Next time I am going to think twice before I act in a moment of anger.

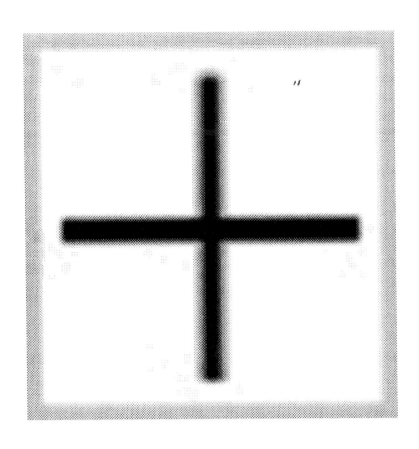

For this very reason, make every effort to add to your faith goodness; and to goodness, knowledge; [6]*and to knowledge, self-control; and to self-control, perseverance; and to perseverance, godliness;* [7]*and to godliness, brotherly kindness; and to brotherly kindness, love.*   *2 Peter 1:5-7*

ADD... Build your life.

While division helps break life into little pieces to more fully examine and ascertain where to grow and subtraction helps deduct negative feelings and actions that could hurt, addition helps build a life that is enjoyable. God desires us to have a good full life *(John 10:10)*. This comes when right desires are fulfilled. God created us to desire Him *(Psalm 40:6-8)*. He created a void in our hearts exclusively for Himself. We can be truly happy when we fill our hearts with Him. We can do this by conducting our lives and growing into who He created us to be. He wants us to grow in His likeness. Build a life that counts by "adding," so when the storms of life rage, you can be sure what you have built will withstand whatever storms may come *(Matthew 7:24)*.

Faith foundation... In *2 Peter 1:5,* faith is already assumed to be there. Personal faith is the foundation upon which a life is built. The faith in Christ you have inherited, explored, sought out, examined, wrestled with and accepted as truth, is what can save you *(Ephesians 2:8)*. Faith is the one ingredient for which God is looking *(Hebrews 11:6)*. While you can not add anything to saving faith, it is through faith you come into a right relationship with God and pass over from death unto life *(Luke 7:50)*. The Christian life is more than just "being saved." What happens after salvation? Faith is so much more than just "fire insurance" and a one-time decision. Salvation is just the beginning! When our daughter was born, it was a great celebration, just like when a person comes to Christ there is a party in heaven *(Luke 15:7)*. But the real work on building a life happens after the baby is born. Once you become "born again" unto God *(John 3:3)*, it is a new beginning into a new life *(2 Corinthians 5:17)*. The new life needs to be built upon. In *1 Corinthians 3:10-15*, Paul shares how a person is "saved" and then builds a life as an "expert builder." Each person's life will be shown and tested for what it is. It is not a question of salvation, but of the quality of life and Christian character. If the builder chases after the wrong things and a life is built on material valuables rather than virtues, that person will suffer loss and lose all he has built *(1 Corinthians 3:15)*. Paul goes on to remind us we are God's temple, and God is building a beautiful sanctuary for Him within the hearts and minds of His people *(1 Corinthians 3:16)*. Addition is about building the temple of God *(us)* into all it can be.

In college, many students put their faith on hold as they solely focus on education, relationships, work, social life or sports. Do not check out, as if you were in a boring class. Do not put your faith on hold! Once you make a faith decision for Christ, do not be "done with it" and become lobotomized to the things of faith. Discover the deeper things of faith and desire the deeper things of God *(1 Corinthians 3:1-3)*. Ask, seek, and knock as you journey in life *(Luke 11:10)*. God's desire is to help you find truth for life *(Proverbs 8:17),* and the best is yet to come. A couple went on a cruise for a week. All week they eyed the fabulous buffets for which cruises are famous. They were so worried about spending money for the buffet, they settled for crackers in their room. At the end of the week, they finally had the courage to ask the price of the buffet, only to find the buffet was included in the cruise. All they had to do was get a plate! Do not settle for the "crackers" of life and faith, but seek and find the fabulous spiritual food God has for you when He paid the price for your salvation.

I am rarely impressed with a group of students; I am usually impressed and proud of individuals. There was a group, five guys and one girl. A couple, with whom this group associated, was driving home from a concert in Austin when a semi-truck lost control and ended up slamming into their car. One of them died, and the other was paralyzed from the waist down. I could not believe the impact this accident had on the school and my students. I was not sure how the students were going to react, but I certainly was not prepared to be blown away by their compassion. Instead of blaming God for the death of their friend, and getting "mad" at Him for allowing the accident, they came closer to each other and God. One morning one of the guys in the group said, "I am so glad that Jacob is still alive and God has given

me the opportunity to minister to him and his family." Another pair of the group shared their thoughts. "This situation has really strengthened my faith. I have to trust God that He knows what He is doing and that Jacob still has a purpose here since he didn't die like Amanda did." The other said, "Amanda is in the presence of God now. That is too cool." The group rallied around the family of Amanda and around Jacob in the weeks after the accident. Talking to them one day, I showed my surprise in their actions. "I am so impressed that you all are drawing closer to God rather than further away from Him during this horrible time." They looked at each other. "Well, it's because we love God so much. We know He has our best intentions at heart. He knows what we can handle." What a firm foundation in Christ they had—and so young. I am still impressed with them.

Add goodness... This is the first addition that builds upon faith. Your faith should always make you a better person. The Gospel is often termed as "Good News." Your faith others might refute. Your arguments others might contest. Your motivations others might question. However, your goodness and good deeds speak for themselves. A good tree is known by it's good fruit *(Matthew 12:33)*. God created you for good works *(Ephesians 2:10),* and as the old song goes, "Jesus loves me when I'm good, when I do the things I should; Jesus loves me when I'm bad, though it makes Him very sad." God wants you to be good, even and especially when no one is looking. From the well of goodness comes happiness and fulfillment in life.

I became a part of the church because the people knew how to have good and healthy fun! They were good to me and I in turn wanted to be a good person. Many students see their faith as a morbid ritual instead of a challenge to goodness. Goodness is a Godly beauty that makes even the harshest skeptic wince. Learn to have good and healthy fun. Enjoy the beauty of goodness. Some say it is no fun being good, but the by-product of being good is a clear conscience, a pure heart, and a freedom no one can take away, unless you allow them.

There are two ways to view humanity: people are either all bad or all good. A mechanic friend viewed all people as jerks who are selfish and rude. He hated and had a guarded preconceived notion of people even before he got to know them. This was influenced by his past negative experiences with people. I, on the other hand, used to think everyone was good-natured, sincere, honest and committed to the ultimate good for all. This was influenced by my past positive experiences with people. Our perspective on the human race depends on our life experiences, and it matters how we interact and respond to other people.

The truth is not everyone is either all bad or all good. When God made humanity, He called it very good *(Genesis 1:31)*. Everyone, however, has done wrong *(Psalm 14:1)*, and everyone has fallen short of goodness *(Romans 3:23)*. We can have traces of goodness and badness, but as "Sons of Adam," we are born into a cycle of innate badness. God came to free us from the bondage of badness when He sent His Son, so that through Him, we might have the chance at tasting goodness. This is not a one-time occasion, but a lifelong affair. God wants us to be good. Instead of peoples' goodness and badness being painted in black and white, there is gray. Sometimes, good people do bad stuff, and bad people do good stuff. Even the vilest of offenders can do good. Acts of goodness are not out of reach for anyone.

There is a formula for goodness: "To act justly and to love mercy and to walk humbly with your God" *(Micah 6:8)*. Because of the bad things we have done, we do not want justice from God. It is His kindness, love and mercy that makes us right with Him *(Titus 3:4-5)*. We want to prove our love for God by loving other people *(Luke 7:47)* so we treat them justly by showing them mercy. It is not for those whom have received mercy to withhold mercy. Give people kindness and love by being good to them. Store goodness in your heart by resting and depending on God's goodness. From a good heart will come good deeds *(Matthew 12:35)*. When in doubt, cling to goodness *(Romans 12:9)*. Try not to hurt others, but always try to do good to all people *(Galatians 6:10)*, even if you can not stand them.

Eddie was a nice guy. He made the class laugh and was always respectful. But Eddie got in to trouble at school, a lot. He left school for lunch even though we have closed campus lunch. He stepped on and broke another student's glasses in the locker room. He walked out of a teacher's class after he was denied permission to go the bathroom. He was late to school fifteen days in six weeks. He skipped school three times. For all these things, he was sent to ISS for a total of three weeks. Meanwhile, the soccer team made it to the finals. It was a big game. The game was in Austin. Since Eddie was in ISS, he was not allowed to attend. If he went, it would result in another demerit, which meant he would have to go to DAEP for the rest of the year and would not be able to partake in prom or graduation ceremonies. That did not stop Eddie. He went to the game anyway. On Monday, back at school, the administration called him to the office, saying they had seen him at the game and he was going to receive another demerit. Eddie repeatedly denied going. A battle ensued involving the school board and his parents. The following Wednesday, the school paper came out. There, on the front page, was a picture of "fans" at the state finals game for soccer. Guess who was in the middle of the stands—Eddie! Needless to say, he was caught in his lie, and was sent to DAEP for the rest of the semester. It was amazing to me that Eddie would get into so much trouble because he was so different in class—it just did not fit with the nice student I knew from first period. Eddie is a good person; he just made some really bad decisions!

Jack and Tyler had received low grades in my class since the first day. I was continually changing the seating chart in their class because the students liked to talk. After one seating chart change, Jake and Tyler seemed to be doing really well! At first I thought it was because I finally found a place that put them away from distractions so they could concentrate on the class work. Boy was I wrong! I started to notice a trend: when Ashley, the girl that sat directly in front of Jack, did well, so did Jack and Tyler. However, when

Ashley did poorly, so did Jack and Tyler. Ahhhhhh…. So I decided to get some proof before I approached them. I made two tests. I gave Jack and Tyler one version. I gave Ashley the other, and just as I expected, their answer sheets were identical. I was disappointed in all three of them: Ashley for letting the guys copy off her, and Jack and Tyler because they were copying. They copied every answer word for word, blank for blank! Not just every now and then, but *all* the time. When I confronted them, they were not happy. Jack had just been accepted on a baseball scholarship and was worried about this tainting his reputation there. Tyler just wanted to graduate so he could go into the Army. Ashley was embarrassed and worried about how her mother would react. I told each of them I would let their failing grades stand, and it would be their decision to make up the difference. They made the right decision—it didn't happen again.

Add knowledge… You go to school to learn and understand. Knowledge is much more than learning and regurgitating information, but the ability to understand. Learn how to grow and make the most of the knowledge you have. Absorb, observe, process and apply what you learn. Intellectual knowledge alone produces liberalism, a head full of structural knowledge, but no heart to apply it. Heart knowledge produces fanaticism, a passionate heart, but with no structural reason. A mixing of the two, the integration of knowledge of heart and head, is wisdom. There are two kinds of wisdom: wisdom that is pure and leads to confidence, and wisdom that "puffs up" and leads to destruction *(James 3:13-18)*. Crave wisdom that makes you a better person, helps you in your everyday struggles and leads you on to being a more consummate person.

Be excited about learning by being "a sponge." Stretch yourself by developing and absorbing information and ideas around you by trying new things: a hobby, a trip, a food or learning how to play a musical instrument. Add newness by putting off the old self and being made new *(Ephesians 4:22-24)*. Do this by sacrificially offering your whole self to God *(Romans*

12:1-2). Practice thinking about spiritual excellence *(Philippians 4:8).* Every day ask yourself, "How can I be wiser, smarter, better?" *(Proverbs 9:9).* If you are like most people, learning and being better does not just happen. If we are going to be better, we need to plan, strategize and make ourselves actually do it on purpose. One way to jump start your growth is to have a personal calendar to write goals, dates and timelines. We often do this for classes and bills. However, when it comes to our personal life and success, we tend to get lackadaisical. We procrastinate and then binge just in the nick of time. Timing is everything. If you can learn to grow and absorb true wisdom a little bit at a time, and discipline yourself to adhere to commendable and beneficial principles of learning, you can begin to master the art of timing.

I worked really hard. I should have been working on my thesis (a 60ish page requirement for graduating with a Masters degree) for several months. But to tell the truth, I only had a rough draft of the first chapter done. I had three more chapters to go; I had just been married; I had a new job to start; I only had three weeks to finish it. I lived with my thesis topic (Dorothy L. Sayers) for those three weeks. My new husband would come home at night. We would eat dinner and talk awhile, then off to my computer I would go. He would go to bed; I would stay up all night working. He would get up to go to work; I would just be laying down for a nap. We went to lunch one day after I had met with my advisor. While we were eating, I spaced out. I just sat, staring into space. I was so deep in thought I was absent from my lunch. I returned to reality when my husband began snapping his fingers. "Hey, Sara, you here? Where'd you go?" I blinked away my thoughts and returned to the salad in front of me. "Oh, sorry; I was just thinking about my paper." Apparently, that was not the only time it happened. During that one lunch alone my husband claims it happened three times! I was consumed in my paper. But all the hard work really paid off. I finished my thesis. I graduated with my Masters Degree. I received a great job as

a result, and the satisfaction of knowing that I have been well educated from one of the best private universities in Texas.

Gaining knowledge is about your stature. *Proverbs 1:1-7* describes wisdom as being open and willing to learn, listen and understand. If you want to learn, you have to be teachable. A well-rounded education does not necessarily have to do with the school you go to, but what you do with the information from your school. How will you react to the knowledge you have been given? Have you ever known someone, where to be around him was an education? Where he intrigued you to be like him? When he talked, you learned from his wisdom; not only from his words, but also from his experiences, attitudes and the way he treated people. In seminary, I lived with a family where I pastored a church on weekends. I learned so much "knowledge" from seminary, but I learned "life-knowledge" from that family. I learned how to be a family man, love my future wife, serve others, help around the house, fight fairly and engage in meaningful conversations. Years later, I do not always quite remember my classes, but I remember that Christian family, and the love they held for each other and for God. Get knowledge you need for school and life.

Add knowledge of maturity by seeking to attain the full measure of God *(Ephesians 4:13)*. In our fatalistic society, we often succumb to the *"Chicken Little Syndrome"* so when something bad happens, we say "the sky is falling." The sky is usually not falling as hard as we think. Maturity combines understanding and perspective. Although gas prices will rise and fall and years of adversity and moments of prosperity come and go, we will survive. God has authority over your situation, and as the old saying goes, "Everything's gonna be alright." It usually will be. Add maturity by being exposed to the complexities of life, while not being swayed from convictions. Seek a fresh and new calling–the voice inside called "vocation" of what you want to do and be. Know the world, your life, your family and your circumstances can and will change. "This is your life." Instead of procrastinating personal assessment by envious "fence looking," remember what you have and what you

59

build is up to you. Do with it what you may. The effect of true knowledge is maturity, and the price of maturity is responsibility. You are responsible for yourself and attaining knowledge can catapult you to maturity.

A fragile student, with whom I deal very carefully, made a 68 on his research paper. I thought about trying to give him more points, so I manipulated his grade to a 70. I knew he would be disappointed, and I was worried he would have a negative reaction. He came to me after I passed out the graded research papers. "Mrs. Welshimer, you are right about the comments on my paper. I did stop working on the last part. I knew the first part was good, but I was worried about the last part. I agree with my grade." I was blown away by his maturity, not blaming me but taking responsibility for his own lack of motivation to work.

    <u>Add self-control</u>... You are only in control of yourself. As much as we would like to think we can control other people, situations, circumstances or even the weather, the truth is we can not, unless that control is given to us. One sure thing, however, is we are in control of ourselves.
    In my life and ministry, I have "Three Rules":
    1. Don't hurt anyone.
    2. Don't hurt anything.
    3. Don't get into trouble.
My experience through life has convinced me that these three rules are a key to self-control. Try not to hurt people, including their feelings, egos, reputations or bodies. Try not to hurt stuff, especially if it does not belong to you. Stay out of trouble, by getting out of a potentially bad situation, refusing to participate in questionable activities or not hanging around the wrong people at the wrong time. There is wisdom in the paternal advice, "There's nothing good that happens after 2:00 am." When you play with trouble, ask yourself, "Is the possible damage irrevocable or irreparable?" "Is it something I can get out of?" Sometimes trouble can be a small thrill, but cost you dearly.

Self-control is a struggle, but the promise of God is He always provides a way out of a situation, although sometimes you have to search for it (*1 Corinthians 10:13*). There is always opportunity to do right, and as you reflect upon yourself, look beyond where you are now. What will life look like down the road? What are you to become? Remember whatever you are going through, "This too shall pass," whether it is good or bad. When it comes to addiction, dating, sex, education, work, finances, fitness, career, relationships or spirituality, be the master of your emotions. No one has power over you, unless you yield power to them, either consciously or unconsciously. This masterful art takes awareness, self-reflection, alertness and stamina. When all about you are losing their heads, keep yours, and endure hardship (*2 Timothy 4:5*). Learn to be patient and control your temper (*Proverbs 16:32*). In the midst of incompetence, ineffectiveness and decay, rise above your circumstances and be wise by controlling yourself (*Proverbs 29:11*).

Harry and Sadie had been dating for a year and a half. They broke up three weeks prior to an incident that took place. Sadie was upset about the break up and wanted to continue dating Harry; Harry felt otherwise. She started saying some mean, cruel things to him, in front of his friends. He had no reaction. He did not get mad; he was not apologetic; he simply stood there, looked her in the eye and remained silent as she talked. This angered her to no end. She slapped him—hard, so hard that when I saw him two hours later, his cheek was still red. Harry did not know what to do. He wanted to lash back at her in his anger of the humiliation he suffered in front of his friends and the pain of the slap he just endured. Instead, he just stood there. He gritted his teeth and stood there. He did not respond at all. This, of course, infuriated Sadie even more. She returned to him, yelling more obscenities, and was quickly taken away by an administrator. When I heard the story, others in the class wondered if his response had been appropriate. I assured him it was. "Harry, you showed a lot of maturity and

restraint. Your apathy is what made her mad. The fact that you controlled your words and actions shows a lot about your character. I am very proud of you." I wish the other students in the room would show half the amount of maturity he showed that day.

Add perseverance... On October 29, 1941, U.K. Prime Minister Winston Churchill visited his alma mater, Harrow School. In his keynote address he said, "Never, never, never, never, never, never give up" and that was it! Simple, yet profound! How tough are you? What is your breaking point? What struggles and mistakes have you made and been through that give you hope to persevere? Are you confident you can make it through life's future challenges? *2 Corinthians 4:7-12* describes the Christian life being "hard pressed, but not crushed; perplexed, but not in despair; persecuted, but not abandoned; struck down, but not destroyed." Ask God for vigor to keep on going, so you can attain the prize both now and in the times to come.

"Work hard, play hard" is the motto of many fraternal organizations. Some people work too hard and do not play, missing out on the joys of relationships, entertainment and rest. Many students play too hard, but forget to work, and they usually have to go home the next semester or pay for it for the rest of their lives. Work hard and play hard by giving 100% in whatever you decide to do. Do not go halfway by slacking in the middle. Remember most endeavors start looking mundane and boring halfway through when the luster of newness wears off. Work hard, even when you do not "feel" like it. Do not let your feelings dictate your work ethic. In faith, in work and in life, there is a prize at the end of the race for what you do and who you are. Never give up!

Lisa was a hard worker. She always had her papers and homework in on time. When she knew she was going to be absent, she would come to me beforehand and get her work done; if she was going to miss a test or quiz, she would make it up before she left. She would bring me her papers

three days before it was due to make sure it was done correctly. Lisa was always prepared, and whether it was a reading assignment or a worksheet, she always had it completed. On the weekends, while her friends were at parties, she would be home finishing up a project that was not due until the next week. Where Lisa was a hard worker, her friend Allie was a slacker. She would party any night of the week. She would visit with friends instead of working on papers. Allie would write a letter or text message a friend before she would finish a homework assignment or read a story she missed while sleeping in class. If she was to be absent, she had to be tracked down to do a missing assignment. One day, I joked about it with them. "If we could get Allie to work a little more and Lisa to slack off just a bit, you all would make the perfect well-rounded person." Allie needed to work a little harder at her school work, whereas Lisa needed to spend some time on the phone instead of reading ahead...again.

Add Godliness... Grow in your relationship with Christ by being spiritual *(Romans 12:1).* Seek out quiet places within your soul to connect with the real you in order to be honest with yourself and with God. God gave *(John 3:16),* and if you want to experience Godliness, give like God. Give cheerfully *(2 Corinthians 9:7).* Give some of your time, energy, attention, resources or love, but do it without expecting to get anything in return. Godliness has great gain and value for all things *(1 Timothy 4:8)* in every area of life. Who do you know that is Godly? How can you imitate that person to become someone whom others might view as Godly?

No one thought badly of Brian. It is rare a student can be friends with everyone, and get on no one's "bad side." That was Brian. He lived his life the way he wanted to—with integrity (he never said negative things about another person); with courage (he was not afraid to stand up for what he believed); with trustworthiness (everyone could trust him to do what he said); with an open mind (he never looked

down on anyone for having a different opinion, though he would openly disagree with them, he was still friendly without letting differences get in the way of his friendship). Brian was a Christian, and everyone knew it; not by what he said, but by the way he lived. Another student, Tom, was different. This student always had a different opinion from everyone else. He dressed differently, and he talked differently. One day he was absent. Some members of the class started talking about how strange Tom was. I was engaged in a conversation with another teacher at the doorway. However, I was listening to the members of the class talking (yes, I was not paying too much attention to my colleague). I was about to put an end to their gossiping when Brian did it for me. "So, he's different. It'd be boring if he was like everyone else, but let's talk about the pep rally Friday. Who is going to paint their faces? Do you think those sophomore girls will wear those funny football-like uniforms again?" I was impressed by Brian's Godly attitude. He not only stood up for Tom, but Brian also put a stop to the gossip.

Add brotherly kindness... In college, you might have a lot of acquaintances, but only a few you can call real friends. A student came to me, depressed, saying he did not have any friends or anyone to do anything with. He felt like no one cared. I asked him whom he is friendly to and with whom he would like to be friends. He spouted off a litany about why he would not want to be friends with the stereotypical people that surrounded him. I told him if he wanted friends, he had to be a friend first. Jonathan and David were best friends because Jonathan loved David as much as he loved himself *(1 Samuel 20:17)*. Seek out good friends that will love you and will return that love. You do not have to be best friends with everyone *(even Jesus had only twelve disciples, and three were closer to Him)*, but you should be kind to everyone.

Some teenagers can be the meanest people in the world. Competitive violence tends to engage students to either master others or dismiss them. When in doubt, be nice, don't be mean!

In sixth grade, an awkward girl named Bridget wore thick glasses, was a little overweight and wore no makeup. She sat behind me in class. She was always inquiring about me and even asking me out. I not only blew her off, but *(as most sixth grade guys do)* made many jokes and rude remarks, often at her expense. The first day of seventh grade, there was a new girl on campus. She was a knock-out that made all of the guys talk. After strategizing all morning about how I would approach her *(and still look cool in front of all my friends),* I went up to her and inquired about her name. She looked at me and said, "It's me, Bridget!" All I could say was "Wow!" Over the summer, she had lost weight, traded her thick glasses for blue contacts and had done her hair and make-up. I will never forget the words she said to me: "You didn't give me the time of day before, and now it's your turn." Vengeance was hers. Be nice to everyone because people change. If you make a habit of burning bridges, it could cost you when you want to eventually cross one.

Be kind to those above you. My trigonometry teacher had a sharp foreign accent. Every time she said, "Please pull out a 'shet' of paper," the whole class snickered. During class, students would ask her to repeat things over and over. Once one person got it, they would translate it for others. This made her feel uncomfortable. Because I struggled in trig, I visited her once a week for help. Although I often did not understand her, I smiled, nodded and thanked her. By the end of the semester, I had worked very hard, and she knew it. While I probably deserved a "C," she gave me an "A." Was it because I was kind to her and treated her like a good teacher? Sometimes it pays to be kind to your teachers.

Be kind by engaging in controversial conversations with people in order to both better understand the complexities of life and disagree without being disagreeable. Brothers and sisters sometimes disagree, argue and even fight *(that's the nature of family),* but they are still family. Be a brother and sister to others by not severing ties just because of differing assumptions or ideas. It is okay to be independent, think for yourself and even disagree; it is not okay to be disagreeable. Be a "team-player" by learning how to lead and follow while being nice about it.

People might not remember what you said, or even what you did, but they will remember how you treated them and how you made them feel. Treat them with "brotherly" *(and sisterly)* kindness.

You never know what a smile and a kind word will do for someone's day. A student in fifth period, Amy, was very quiet. She was shy. Though she was American, she acted like a foreigner. Her parents had been missionaries in China her entire life. She grew up there, speaking Chinese and attending a school with Chinese students. As a junior, her parents had returned to the United States. She was in culture shock her first years here, and was having a hard time speaking and writing her native language and understanding her teenage peers. I always smiled at Amy when she entered my classroom and said hello to her. Even that type of attention would make her blush and look around timidly as she would respond in a quiet way. Though she did well in my class, she was always hesitant about asking me questions because she was so shy. One day, Amy left her art portfolio in my class. She came back during lunch to pick it up and I asked her if I could see some of her work. She was an incredible artist. Her paintings and creations were unlike anything I had ever seen from a teenager. I praised her and her work. Other than that one encounter, I never spoke to her for longer than just a few seconds at the beginning of class when I greeted her everyday as she walked in the door. The next year I was blown away when I received an email from her mother. Amy had gone to college and written an essay on an influential person in her life. Amy's topic for her paper was me. She wrote about how my one personal greeting was a highlight in her day. She also wrote about how depressed she had been upon her return to the States and that I was a bright spot in her otherwise bleak days at an American high school. The paper addressed that one encounter with her when I praised her artwork; apparently, this had given her the courage to pursue a career in Art. Wow! All that just because I was nice to her for a few seconds at the beginning of class.

Moving in the middle of your senior year can not be easy. I am always sad for students that have to leave their friends, and sometimes their families, for one reason or another and start over at a new high school so close to graduation. Richard came to my school right after Christmas. The circumstances in his changing schools were beyond his control, but how he took the integration into his new school was not. Richard was always so nice to people. He would laugh with them and find silly things to talk about with anyone. Once he asked a group why girls liked to eat yogurt. Other topics he brought up included people talking during a movie or whether people brought their lunch to school or ate in the lunchroom. His composure and ease of making others feel comfortable won him many friends. Soon he was known all over school. He chose to make the best of his situation just by being nice to the people around him.

Add love... Many students do not love themselves. They view themselves poorly and live destructively, by picking up habits and attitudes that could lead to their demise. Learn to love yourself. God created you to be the person you are with all of your gifts and graces. God made you wonderfully in His own image *(Psalm 139:13-14)*. As the old saying goes, "God don't make no junk." Love yourself by taking care of yourself, reflecting on your life, guarding your heart and body from impurity and building a life of which you can be proud. When we love ourselves, we are more capable of loving others. The great "love chapter" in *1 Corinthians 13* shares what love is: "patience, kindness, protecting, trusting, hoping, persevering, never failing, not self-seeking, not easily angered, not boastful or proud or envious, and love keeps no record of wrongs." Love yourself by not beating yourself up because you are not like someone else or do not have the same opportunities or things that other people have. Love yourself so you can love others, but do so deeply *(1 Peter 4:8)*. We throw around the word love: I love chocolate, that car, that sport, a person or even God. But love can be so much more than a fleeting moment. True love might cost you something, make you hurt or your heart pump faster, but that love can change your life and the world. God loved *(John 3:16)*. Because of this love, we can experience the ecstasy of His love in our relationships and lives.

Love by being humble. "A person's pride might bring him low, but a humble person gains honor*" (Proverbs 29:23)*. "Humility comes before honor" *(Proverbs 15:33)*. Love your life by humbly accepting it as it comes, and enjoying each day and experience as a gift from God. How intriguing and perplexing it is that better people have gone before us who do not have this day to live, love and enjoy. Count your blessings. Do not put all of your confidence in your flesh *(Philippians 3:3)* or in the things of this world. They too shall pass one day, be taken away or can be harshly criticized. Humble love will be remembered and can never be taken away *(1 Corinthians 13:13)*. No one is invincible, and we can all be replaced. So do not take yourself too seriously. Learn to laugh at yourself and the world *(Proverbs 17:22)*, while holding God's love deep within your heart.

Gil was always in a rush. One day I saw him in the hallway during class. He was nearly running down the hall. I had to call out to him twice for him to stop and come talk to me. I asked him what class he was in. "Algebra." I made a face; I am an English teacher. "Yuck. What a boring class. I guess you're going to take your time getting back to class, huh? Gonna go to the bathroom in the Athletic Building?" I joked, referring to the furthest point on campus. "Oh no, I gotta get back!" He started walking away. "I can't miss class!" Off he went. Gil got to school every morning at 6:30. Why? Because he had to be there. He waited in his car for the school to open at 7:00, during which time he would radio truck drivers. When the building opened, he would help out in the library. Why? Because he wanted to. Gil also helped in the Technology Lab, the Content Mastery Room, the Foods and Nutrition and the Broadcasting classes. No, he was not taking any of those classes for credit, he just had to be doing something. Gil did not get along with people

because of the way he dressed; he wore some outrageous things. He did not get along with people because of the way he talked; frankly, his words got mixed up and he was confusing. He did not get along with people because he scored academically well; he struggled in a lot of his classes. He did not get along with people because he was good looking; he was kind of a gangly looking guy with big 80's type glasses. People got along well with Gil because Gil was comfortable with who he was. He had accepted he wanted to be involved with everything. He had accepted he liked to be in a rush all the time. He had accepted himself. And that encouraged people around him. They admired his integrity and his ability to not conform to those around him, but to just be himself.

For if you possess these qualities in increasing measure, they will keep you from being ineffective and unproductive in your knowledge of our Lord Jesus Christ.　　　*2 Peter 1:8*

MULTIPLY... You can be more!
    Multiply in increasing measure... Fire can be good or bad. It is either increasing or decreasing. Fire multiplies in increasing measure or dies in decreasing measure. It can warm, cook food and give light, but it can also burn, destroy and hurt. Fire seems to be a central theme in Scripture.

Check out some Biblical references:
In the Old Testament, fire was a sign from God...
- Our God is a "Consuming Fire" *(Deuteronomy 4:24).*
- The Garden of Eden was guarded by a flaming sword *(Genesis 3:24).*
- Wrath destroyed Sodom and Gomorrah *(Genesis 19:23-25).*
- Moses saw flames from within a burning bush *(Exodus 3:2).*
- God's people were given a pillar of light to lead them *(Exodus 13:21).*
- On Mt. Carmel, God sent fire as a witness for Elijah against the Baal prophets *(1 Kings 18:38).*
- Elijah went up to heaven on a Chariot of Fire *(2 Kings 2:11).*
- Shadrach, Meshach, and Abednego were saved from the fires *(Daniel 3:25).*
- A Refiner's Fire is how God spurns us on to righteousness *(Malachi 3:2-4).*

In the New Testament, fire was a sign from God as well...
- Our God is a "Consuming Fire" *(Hebrews 12:29).*
- You are the light of the world *(Matthew 5:14-16).*
- Hell is filled with fire *(Matthew 5:22).*
- On the Road to Emmaus the disciples asked, "Were not our hearts burning within us?" *(Luke 24:32).*
- Fan into flame the gift of God *(2 Timothy 1:6).*
- At Pentecost, they saw tongues of fire *(Acts 2:3).*
- Judgment is tested with fire *(1 Corinthians 3:13).*
- The lake of fire is the second death *(Revelation 20:14).*
- Jesus said: "I have come to bring fire on the earth!" *(Luke 12:49).*

- And "I am the light of the world. Whoever follows me will never walk in darkness, but will have the light of life" *(John 8:12).*

In the Old Testament, fire is an outward sign. In the New Testament, fire is an inward sign. Some people talk about coming to God because they have "seen the light." I came to God because I have felt the "fires of life."

Right now, you are creating sparks and little fires of passion with your habits, learning skills, education and relationships. What will they look like when they are in full flame as they come to fruition during the next years? Will it be something that warms you or burns you? Remember, in today's world, the fire is inward, not outward. What fires are kindling within your spirit? What is the burning desire of your soul?

The sparks you feed right now will multiply and compound in the future. It only takes a little spark to turn into a roaring fire. The question is: are you feeding the right fire? Education, relationships, money, time and hard work gain interest throughout the years. Multiplying them now can be your nest egg or your downfall.

Consider what and how you will multiply in increasing measure by growing from everything. Find learning points and redemptive qualities in movies, books, music, relationships, classes, TV shows, sermons and life experiences. It seems easy to focus on the negative. That negativity tends to multiply faster than a positive outlook. It is harder to focus on the positive. "There's a silver lining in every cloud" is true, but you must look for it. The energy you spend doing this, will multiply and increase, not only now, but as it compounds for years to come.

Samantha loved to draw. One day I explained in class the eagle was my favorite animal. Soon after, I noticed Sam was drawing a picture of an eagle. I commented on how beautiful the drawing was. "Thanks. I love to draw. My favorite animal is an eagle too." Why? "Because an eagle is free and can fly away from all of life's complexities." That answer bothered me a bit, coming from someone so young. "What

73

exactly do you mean?" She sighed. "I want to go to a special art school in Atlanta next year." As usual, I jumped in and interrupted her, telling her I knew the one. A friend of mine from high school had gone to this elite art school. I was impressed she had been accepted—only a select few from the country were accepted every year. I was guessing the "complexities of life" she referred to earlier had to do with money. "So, you do not have the money to attend?" I questioned. "Not really; I just know that I can't make any money majoring in art. So, I'm going to go to UT and major in business instead. Then maybe one day I will be able to pick up art again." I was confused; her "complexities of life" were majoring in something that could potentially make her wealthy, but not fulfill her emotionally. "Sam, my friend Jason has an art degree from the same school you are discussing and he has a fabulous job in Chicago working for an advertising company. He makes twice as much money as I do and he is younger than I. Start now in doing what you want to do, and you will be surprised at how it will fulfill the passions of your heart. You do not want to do something just for more money when you will be unhappy the rest of your life. The fire to be an artist is in you—pour lighter fluid on it girl, don't put it out."

Multiply by being better, greater, more … You are not stuck. Whatever your plot in life is, you can change it. It might mean hard work, more education, painstaking discipline or even difficult decisions, but you can change if you want. The choice is up to you. You are in charge of your life. Some people have a *"Victim Mentality."* Everything bad is everyone else's fault. It is a sad way to go through life: blaming everyone and everything else for what happens, and then expecting and depending on someone else to fix it. This "victim mentality" creates a "chip on the shoulder" that can paralyze you into ineffective and unproductive living. You can develop negative attitudes like "if only this had happened," "it's all their fault," or "I've been wronged by someone so my life is ruined." Do not buy into being dependent on your situation or circumstances for your happiness or sadness. You can be and do better than that.

God has given us motivation and confidence within His promises because He wants us to be more. What other people do and say might affect us, but we are in control of ourselves and God has authority over our situation. Are you motivated to "multiply" by being more in your life? Do you have confidence God has a wonderful plan for you and you can live life to the fullest with Him? Strive to do better. Instead of just leaves or brush to put on the fire of your heart, strive to put logs on those embers. Build a fire that will keep you warm and sustain you in the cold nights of the soul. Seek humble confidence you are on the right path and your sparks will soon create a wonderful fire that can guide, protect and help you.

Two of my former students participated in a college overseas program to satisfy their language requirement. Jonna was outgoing and very bubbly, while Cynthia was quiet and more focused on her class work. I was excited for their opportunity to go to Mexico. Once there, they would attend classes in order to learn the language and history of the country. The students usually stayed in local homes to absorb the culture. Cynthia and Jonna were roommates in the home of the Rameriz family. Upon their return, I was surprised by the outcome of their time in Mexico. Jonna was intimidated by the Mexican heritage and language. Although she attended class, she stuck with her American friends from college. She ate with them, exclusively chatted with them and spent most of her free time watching American TV and emailing her friends and family in the States. Cynthia, on the other hand, immersed herself in the Mexican culture. She ate dinner with the Rameriz family every chance she got, making good friends with their teenage daughter. She reached out to the teenage daughter's friends, going to Spanish movies and popular restaurants. She spent her free time reading books about Mexican history and watching Spanish TV. She promised herself she was not going to speak English at all while she was there, even refusing to do

so with her American friends. I was impressed with Cynthia's passion to be better by learning the language and understanding the culture; I was disappointed in Jonna selling herself short because she might have been a little uncomfortable.

Fifth period, right after lunch, the students are always kind of crazy, so I allow them a few more minutes to talk before settling them down for the day's work. But this year's fifth period seemed a little more out of hand than usual. The ring leader of it all was a popular baseball player named Brandon. He would engage others in conversation, write notes to his friends and make rude comments about the class work. I struggled to keep him from running the class, but was not sure how to make him settle down. I shared my classroom with his baseball coach. One day I fleetingly spoke to him about Brandon's behavior in class. "Brandon can't seem to keep quiet," I told his coach, "he likes to talk a whole lot, and frankly, it's becoming disruptive." I was not sure what happened that day at practice, but the next day Brandon came into class, put his head down on his desk and only raised it when the class began. He never once opened his mouth unless it was in response to something I asked him directly. This happened every day. The class was exceptionally better; there was less tension between me and the students, and other students had a chance to express themselves without fear of what Brandon would do or say. Near the end of the year, I asked Brandon what made him decide to change his classroom behavior. "Simple," he said, "coach told me that if I opened my mouth in your class again I was off the team. I stopped talking because my passion for baseball exceeded my passion for acting out in this class."

Multiply by yielding... There is a ropes course where participants are blindfolded and instructed to hold onto a rope. The blindfolded members of the group are left alone holding the rope, without any further instruction. Their objective is to find the end of the rope while still holding onto it *(at all times)*. The trick is the rope is in a circle, and there is no end. The solution is to ask the leader for help. Participants go in circles, get perplexed and desperately try to get out of the rope *(sometimes for hours, literally)*, all the while trying to figure out the point of the lesson. Once they do ask for help, the members can take off the blindfolds and are allowed to let go of the rope. Participants usually feel silly at how easy the exercise seems. In life, when you are going in circles and it seems like there is no end to your rope *(again, literally)*, ask for help in order to better your situation.

When you go down the wrong road in life it may seem you have hit either rock bottom or a glass ceiling. Have courage to yield yourself to someone or something to reach your goals and your destiny. John was asked if he was "the Christ," and he knew he was not, so he yielded to Jesus saying, "He must become greater and I must become less" *(John 3:30)*. When you have done all you can do with what you have and still feel stuck, ask for help. Ask God to help find your way by putting people in your life to help you. He promises to come through for us if we will seek Him *(Matthew 6:33)*. Multiply by yielding and asking for help. All kinds of people and resources can help us multiply if we will be open and ready to accept help. Jesus yielded his life by dying on a cross to save those who trust in Him. He yielded to a higher authority *(God the Father)* and chose God's plan for his life.

Scott had mediocre grades in my class. He always did his work, but not to the best of his ability. Research paper time came around. If students do not turn in the paper, they will not be able to pass which may put them in jeopardy of not graduating. There are six due dates for research assignments before the final project is due. Scott had not turned in one of these assignments, so I was worried he would not turn in the final project. Each day I asked him if he needed to go to the library to do research; he always answered in the negative. Two days before the project was due, I called his mother. His mother explained to me Scott had never written a research paper and was intimidated by

the assignment. He was so worried about it he had contemplated suicide the night before. "This project is not worth his life. Why didn't he just come ask me for help? I have said all along I will give extra help to anyone who needs it. He could come to me after or before school if he did not want to do so in front of his friends," I told his mom. Apparently, he was just embarrassed. I pulled Scott aside that day and explained I had no idea he was having so much trouble with the project and he needed to come and ask for help if he wanted it. I definitely relayed the message the project for this class was not worth his life.

I was frustrated with Andrew. Sometimes he would turn in assignments, sometimes he would not. Sometimes he would stay awake in class, but most of the time, he would sleep. Sometimes he would engage in conversation, and sometimes he would sit and sulk. I was frustrated with his apathy toward his performance in class, mostly because I liked Andrew. He was a funny, respectful individual who had so much potential. I talked to him many times about his change in attitude, and he always pushed me aside. This made me think he did not care. How wrong I was. Talking with a few of the other students I found out about Andrew. Andrew's mother had died when he was young. His father liked to show how tough he was by beating Andrew up. Andrew's attitude in class directly reflected the previous evening with his father. If the night had gone well, Andrew was in a good mood, but if the night had gone badly, Andrew was in a bad mood. I talked to his counselor and learned if he had been 17, the state could get involved, but because he was 18 and was "of age" this situation was out of our league. He could have lived anywhere else, but he chose to stay with his father, and why not? It was his father who provided everything for him—a place to stay, a car to drive, money to spend and a reason to be in a good or bad mood. All I could do for Andrew was pray. I yielded to God and prayed for Andrew everyday that year and continue to do so now.

Multiply by multitasking... Life moves pretty fast, and there is always a lot to do in little time. Learn to juggle many things at the same time without dropping anything, by multitasking. When firefighters fight big forest fires, they can either focus on the little fires that pop up or the big central fire that feeds the little ones. When they put all their water on the little fires instead of the big one, it does not help. The big fire will continue to get out of control and spark little ones no matter how much water the firefighters put on them. When this happens, their work seems futile and they will eventually get burned. Instead, when they focus on the big fire, the firefighters lessen the heat from the big fire. While the little fires might come close to burning them, they will eventually putter out because the little fires are no longer fed by the heat of the big fire. The reason why the firefighters achieve victory is because they focus on the big fire first. Focus on the big fires first, and the little ones will be easier to manage.

Prioritize your life by multitasking and knowing which central fire feeds the little fires. I hope you have a big central fire in your life that drives your little fires. Do not focus on the little fires while neglecting the big fire so as to get burned. The little fires matter, for they come from the big fire. Multiply by having many little fires that come from the big fire in your life. If you have been given a gift, a talent, a passion or a trade, much will be required of you *(Luke 12:48)*. Hopefully, it will continue to multiply. Learn to discipline yourself to focus on the big fires of life while tending to the small ones *(1 Corinthians 9:19-27)*. In class, be a student; in sports, be an athlete; in relationships, be a lover; in finances, be an accountant; with your friends, be a friend; in church, be a theologian; in crisis, be a counselor; with family, be an encourager.

Each year teachers are given the opportunity to give an award to a student they feel epitomizes the paragon student. This year, I had to give it to Janice. Though she was on the track team, involved with an elite spirit club, a member of student council, a member of a group that helped at elementary schools and an active member of her youth

group, she still found time to focus on her studies. She was always positive about school rules and functions. She was a friend to absolutely everyone, even helping those who struggled in math and doing unlovely tasks in the cafeteria. She was respectful to all her teachers and the school administration. She had a deep belief in God about which she was not afraid to speak, but was open-minded enough to listen to another's views. I was impressed with Janice. She was involved with so many things, went on retreats with one club or group, and still managed to be in the top ten percent of her class. "How do you do it?" I asked her. "I just find time for everything. I guess God gave me the gift of multitasking," she laughed. Yes, Janice, it seems He did.

Some students think they are busy and under much pressure which is true for many of them, but they do not find much sympathy from me. Though I try to relate to my students, I want them to try to relate to me, too. Erin came to class tired. She was complaining about a phone call she received from her friend at 2:00 in the morning. She stayed on the phone with him until 3:30, so of course, she was tired when the time came to wake up for school. She tried to get sympathy from me. "That's nothing," I retorted. "Just wait until your two year old wakes up from a nightmare at 1:00 when you just went to bed at 11:00 because of your baby's 10:00 feeding. Then, when you finally settle her down and fall back asleep, your baby wakes up at 2:00 because she needs a diaper change. When you finally get her back to sleep at 3:30, your alarm goes off at 5:30 because you have to give your two year old her medicine. Then you wonder if it is worth going back to bed for thirty minutes before you have to get up for work. Try this not one just one night, but two weeks in a row." Erin shook her head. "Well," she tried another subject with me. "I am so busy having to stay up with my homework and having play rehearsal every night for two hours." Again, I could not be convinced to help her out. "Well, try getting home at 4:30 every day, taking care of your kids, getting them dinner, getting them baths and to bed, and then having to stay up for three hours grading really bad research papers. Not to mention the time I cleaned up the kitchen, washed and folded two loads of laundry, did the bills and counseled a troubled friend on the phone for twenty minutes." She realized she was not going to win. "You are busy, Erin," I reassured her. "But enjoy your responsibility-free life while you can. Just wait until next year when you leave home and go to college!"

Multiply by living... Live like today was your last, but plan like you will live forever. Life is fleeting. The future is not promised. You could live a long life, or you could die tomorrow. Life and death is a mystery, and we do not know how, when, or what will be our end, but we can be ready for it.

Multiply by living like you are ready to die. Paul describes our end as a "thief in the night" *(1 Thessalonians 5:2).* In this description, one is usually caught off-guard, sleeping in the night. But if we are prepared, we will treat that thief differently. Be expectant and ready *(Luke 12:40)* when that day comes by multiplying your life. Whenever and whatever may be your end, end on a good note. Say the things that need to be said now. Do the things you want to be remembered for and have "perfect moments." Be ready for the afterlife by searching your soul in this life. The end thing is really the main thing.

Emry and Chris are two students I will never forget. They are the kind of students that keep me coming back every year to teach. They were very kind to this middle aged preacher's daughter and I feel lucky to have been the recipient of their gifts. It was my second year teaching and I became pregnant with my first child. The girls, Emry and Chris, were interested in my changing body, new emotions and the movements of the life inside me. They would often come to my class in order to hear the latest in my pregnancy saga. I enjoyed having them to talk to, since it was all new to me as well. We laughed a lot about stretch marks, expanding stomachs and other things we promised we would never repeat. One day my teacher friend came to me and asked me

to walk to the mailroom with her in order to help her carry some things back to her room. I was actually a little annoyed because I wanted to get home early that day, but of course I conceded to help her. Walking by the cafeteria, I saw balloons and many of my students. It took me a few minutes to realize they were all there for me. A surprise baby shower...for their English teacher. And there in the middle of it all was Emry and Chris. What a perfect moment I never will forget.

Shine is the Discipleship Now weekend at my church. A dear friend of mine, Ginger, and I led a group of girls for the last three years. We were looking forward to another year. This year she was equally excited because the girls were coming to her house. We planned, bought gifts and prepared Bible studies. We were ready. It was so much fun. The first night we had a scavenger hunt set up for the girls around town. It ended with the group having dinner at a restaurant. One girl, Charity, was in a wrestling match for her school that night. She had been trying to catch up with the group for over an hour due to our changing destinations. Finally, she caught up with us at a restaurant. Though it was after 10:30 when she showed up, and she had to return to her match the next morning at 8:00, she still wanted to be there with us that night. She shared a lot with us that weekend. She shared how happy she was her dad had made a decision for Christ. She had been praying for him to become a Christian for two years. He finally made a decision for Christ. Her heart had also been heavy for a good friend of hers who was going through a very tough time, and was possibly suicidal. Charity had spent countless hours with her friend, sharing Christ's love and assuring the friend He could help him. I will never forget some of her words. "I am proud of how I am handling the situation right now. Every time I leave my friend, I am afraid it will be the last time I see him. So I want to say everything I can about how much he means to me, and his family and about God's love for him. I want to have a clear conscience if he does do something to

82

himself." Four months later, Charity died in a tragic car accident. Her death left a void in the world, but I am positive she met her Lord with a clear conscience and no regrets.

Multiply by living and planning like you are ready to live forever. You have a promising future, and most likely, you will live a long life. Are the decisions you make today going to complement or destroy your future in five to ten years? Many times we focus on the temporary and present instead of the permanent and future. What benefits will you reap in the future because of what you do today? *(Galatians 6:7-8).* The long-term might require sacrifice, while the short-term might be easier, but what will help you in the long-run?

Sam came to our school in the middle of the first semester. He was ecstatic that our school had off campus lunch for an entire hour. Sam's behavior was erratic. Some days he would come in bouncing off the walls; others he would fall asleep. However, it was not until he came in calm and delayed I suspected he was doing something illegal during that hour at lunch. We were taking a quiz. I passed out the papers and Sam reached for them—two inches to the right of where I was holding them. He then heard me tell him to take out a sheet of paper, and he sat there for thirty seconds. "Sam? Did you hear me?" He said he thought he had taken it out. His behavior was like that for half the period before he essentially passed out on his desk. I was so disappointed. If only he could see how this "little fun" was affecting his entire future.

Mickey Mantle, the great New York Yankee baseball player, said when he reached 50 years of age: "If I had known I was going to live this long, I would have taken better care of my body!" Your body is a temple of God *(1 Corinthians 6:19),* and the daily decisions you make now will show in the years to come. Brushing your teeth, eating healthy, exercising, reading, abstaining from promiscuity, curtailing addictions and using suntan lotion are simple little things that might require short-term discipline for long-term health.

June was not obese, she was just a bit overweight. I always saw her eating some sort of candy and drinking a Coke. "There's nothing else like a Snickers and a real Coke," she would say. When the class was having donuts, she would eat at least three. When the class was having a party, she would have two of every cookie and a huge piece of the cake with the real icing. "Not that whipped low fat stuff, I like the fat-filled sugar stuff," she would say. She was never uncomfortable with her weight or her eating habits until she was diagnosed with diabetes. June was lucky; there was a chance she would not have to take insulin shots for the rest of her life. If she could control her diet and exercise, she could control her diabetes. June did. She stopped eating sugary things, "Except for my occasional Snickers and Diet Coke now," she boasted. She walked three miles a day, every day because she chose to live. She was determined to be disciplined for her long-term health and existence. She does not mind that her clothes fit much better, too.

<u>**Multiply by praying and working**</u>... Pray like it depends on God, but work like it depends on you. I know a youth minister who prays at least two hours every morning with his staff. While his prayer life is amazing, when I ask him to go and minister at the schools with me, he claims he does not have time because he is in meetings all day. Another youth minister does great things, but when I ask about his "walk with God," he sadly shares he has not personally talked with God in years. While the picture of these two ministers is polarized, God wants us to pray and work, not just settle for one or the other.

God wants you to be fulfilled in both who you are *(found in prayer)* and what you do *(your "good works")*. Pray continually *(1 Thessalonians 5:17),* but work while you pray. My wife's best friend is Jewish. Her dad *(a Baptist Minister)* once said a blessing over her friend's son. My wife wondered if her friend was going to be offended by this "blessing" from

Christianity. Her friend replied, "My son needs all the prayer and blessings he can get!" Pray for your friends, family, church, community, even the world, but be ready on all occasions *(Colossians 4:5)*. You never know when God will summon those who are "in-tune" with Him to great tasks.

Prayerfully look for opportunities to receive and give the gifts of God. There is an old "preacher's joke" about a flood coming into a town, and a man praying God would save him. As the inches of water started to turn into feet, a man in a Hummer pulled up and said, "Hurry, they've evacuated the city and I'm here to save you!" The man replied, "No thanks, God's going to save me!" As the waters continued to creep up, he climbed to the second floor of his house. A boat came by, and the captain said, "Jump in, I'm here to save you!" The man replied, "No thanks, God's going to save me!" As the waters continued to rise, he had to climb up on his roof; there, a helicopter extended a ladder, and the voice came down, "Grab the ladder, I'm here to save you!" The man replied a third time, "No thanks, God's going to save me!" As the waters rose, the man met his fate. At the pearly gates, this man asks God, "I prayed that you would save me from the flood, but why didn't you?" God replies, "I tried, three times: with a Hummer, a boat, and a helicopter!" Pray to God to save you, but look for the everyday practical ways in which He gives opportunities.

I do not want any student to fail my class. I am willing to work with students who are struggling. The problem is some students are not willing to work with me. Josh did not like to work. He would not turn in assignments, study for tests or do simple worksheets that would boost his grade. Because of this trend, he ended up with a failing grade the first two six weeks. I pulled him aside time and time again and encouraged him to come in for tutoring, ask me for help and to study in order that he might receive a passing grade. I told him I would help him memorize vocabulary words. But, he never came in. I told him I would review him for major test. But he never responded. I told him he could do extra writing assignments. But he blew me

off. The last six weeks ended and he had a 62—missing the 70 passing mark. I could never understand why he would go to such great lengths to fail. I contacted his parents several times. I pleaded with his counselor to encourage him. I even sent him down to the principal on a few occasions. He was passing all his other classes, but it was just English he did not want to pass. To this day, I feel like I gave him every opportunity to save his grade, but his apathy is what kept him from graduating with his friends. I still do not understand.

Multiply by preparing... The Boy Scout motto is "Be Prepared." At a campout, we started playing midnight capture the flag. Although it was not forecasted, it not only started raining, but it poured. I thought the game was going to be over, but the rain just made the game much more fun. The guys were ready for it. After we were thoroughly soaked down to our socks and each team had won numerous games, it was time to get warmed up at the campfire. Everything was wet, but one guy had dipped his matches in wax so they were waterproof. He was prepared for the rain and because of his preparations, we were warmed by the campfire. God wants us to "be prepared" for the rainy times of life, so we too can be warmed by His fire in the dark, wet and cold nights of the soul. We can "be prepared" by being ready *(Luke 12:39-40)* with our souls for every occasion, by preparing our minds, being self-controlled *(discipline),* and setting our hope in God *(1 Peter 1:13).* You can be prepared for the different seasons of life by hiding God's Word in your heart *(2 Timothy 4:2, Psalm 119:11).* Have you prepared your heart, soul, mind and body for the days to come, whether sun or rain? As in the campfire, preparations are everything, especially when you are in the dark and in need of some warmth. We do not and can not know the future, but we can be ready for what may come by being prepared.

God has prepared a place for the Christian *(John 14:2-3).* God desires us to commit whatever our preparations are to Him *(Proverbs 16:3).* He promises He will direct our steps *(Proverbs 16:9).* What are you doing to prepare for the future? What preparations have you made for your soul, your family, your education and your future? Are you ready for whatever may come? Do you rest in the promise God has a place prepared for you?

Kellene had a difficult time hiding her emotions. If she had a bad day, it was written all over her demeanor. If she had a good day, her smile was enough to conquer the world. When it came to grades, she was serious. On test days, she would come in one of two ways. If she came in calm and relaxed, I would point out the importance of the test's grade to her average. "Oh, I know. I am not worried. I studied the Character Chart, Mrs. Welshimer. I am confident that I will ace this test." Some test days, however, she would come into class nervous and looking for someone else's notes to look over. Again, I would point out the importance of the day's test grade. Sweating, she would glance at me hurriedly, "Mrs. Welshimer, don't say that! I stayed up all night on the phone with my boyfriend and didn't study!" By the end of the semester, I did not have to say anything to her to find out if she had studied for a test or not. I told her about my observation of her character. She laughed. "I hate not being prepared. I worry about it so much when I'm not ready for a test that I have nightmares about it. It controls my thoughts and actions to the point of exhaustion! But when I am prepared, I feel so good! I can focus on all sorts of other things because I know that I'm ready for the test so I don't have to fret about it!"

<u>Multiply by sharing your faith</u>… Your faith should always build up, help and make you and other people better, because faith is about joy, hope, love, grace and the Divine entering into our lives. I love salt on everything because frankly, it makes everything taste better. Jesus says "you are the salt of the earth" *(Matthew 5:13)*. As salt, you should make everything better because of the faith you have. Our faith gives taste in a tasteless world, because faith is always about "Good News."

One year we took our youth group to the beach for a couple of hours. None of us thought we would get sunburned since we were only there for a short period of time. When we came back, everyone was deeply sunburned except one person. He said before he went out, he lathered up with sunscreen. He visited there last week and knew he would get sunburned if he did not. We asked him why he did not share that timely information with all of us. He replied, "No one asked, and I didn't think anyone cared." Well, we did care, even though we did not ask. We were sore and blistered for days to come because of the severity of our burns. Many people seem to be burning all around us, and we have the "spiritual sunscreen" that can help and protect. It is not our job to apply the sunscreen, but to offer it, even if nobody seems to care.

Have a full understanding not only by absorbing and digesting your faith, but sharing it *(Philemon 6)* in big and small ways. It is one thing to learn it, but it is a whole different ball game to share it. Multiply by sharing your faith with good ideas, helpful works, acts of mercy, kind words and well-articulated, thought-out conversations.

Her senior year at a new school had not been easy for her. She had not made friends easily. Having to live in a foster home because her parents were incapable of taking care of her did not help the situation. Her first papers were deeply emotional and mainly about her hardships. She dressed attractively, but conservatively. I never heard her engage in gossip of any kind or use any foul language. Emmy told me one day she was a Christian and she wanted her faith to be not just in word, but in deed as well. Throughout the year, though, something happened to her. Her papers became shallow and materialistic. She started dressing a little more conspicuously. When she talked in low whispers in class, I often heard her degrading other students, very colorfully. It all culminated when she was caught doing drugs in the bathroom, of all places, during school. She was reprimanded and put in DAEP for six weeks. She came back from DAEP the same way she left, completely opposite of the

Emmy I had come to know at the beginning of the year. One day, a student of mine, Eric, came to me while the class was working on a group project. Emmy's desk being near mine allowed her to overhear our conversation. Eric told me how he had been to a retreat the weekend before with a friend's church and how the weekend had a large impact on him spiritually and emotionally. "The last night I accepted Jesus Christ as my personal Lord and Savior. I had never really listened to Jesus' plea to come to Him before because of all the hypocrites I've met. There are so many people I know that profess to be believers, but their lives don't match their faith. This weekend I realized people who act that way have problems, but that is not what Christianity is all about. I did accept Christ as my Savior, but I also made a commitment not to act like those Christians I see as hypocrites." We had a wonderful conversation. I was so happy for him and impressed with his maturity about the decision he had made. Emmy was absent the next two days, and upon her return on Monday, she came to my room before school started. She explained that Eric not being afraid to talk to me so openly about his decision had become a turning point in her life. "I am not sure what happened to me this year," she explained, "but everything Eric said about the people he hated was me. He talked to you openly, in the middle of class, not scared about the people around him that could've been listening. He wasn't scared about it at all. I took a good look at my life, and after making myself physically sick for two days, I finally surrendered my misdirection to God." I bet Eric will never know the impact he had on Emmy.

Though the law keeps me from saying a lot of things I would like in front of my class and my students, I still take every opportunity I can to share my faith. While I am not allowed to directly preach to them, I look for other indirect ways to share how God has impacted my life. Luckily, students pretend to be interested enough in my life to try to get me off subject while I teach. Instead of reading, they love to hear a story about my two young girls, what I was like in high school, relationships in college or even just funny everyday happenings. Though students think they have "won" when they succeed in getting me "off topic," I allow it to happen at times because it is my chance to share my faith. "So, Mrs. Welshimer, how many times did you get drunk in high school?" What a great opportunity to tell students how I did not think drinking was appropriate and how I did not even have my first drink until I was 22 because the law said it was wrong until then. I also tell them I do not want to drink now because I do not want to cloud my vision when taking care of my two young girls. "Were you popular? What group did you hang out with?" are questions I get all the time. I tell the students I had friends from all sorts of groups. I spent a lot of time with my youth group doing ministry work, and people from all sorts of schools and groups joined me. The one I undoubtedly get every year: "How old were you when you lost your virginity?" The answer is easy and one I hope someone takes to heart. "May 26th, 2001. The day I got married."

Multiply by bearing fruit... As a tree is known by it's fruit and a good tree bears good fruit *(Matthew 7:17),* you will be known by who you are and what you do. How are you doing in the fruit section? In the categories of the "fruit of the Spirit" in love, joy, peace, patience, kindness, goodness, faithfulness, gentleness and self-control *(Galatians 5:22-23),* where are you ripe? Where do you need to grow? What are you known for? What do other people see? What of your fruit have you allowed other people to taste?

To multiply by bearing fruit, you must be connected to the vine *(John 15:1-17).* A branch connected to the vine has the sources available to grow, produce and bear fruit, even if it is pruned once in a while. But if the branch is not connected to the vine, it withers and becomes a stick, only to be thrown into the fire. Be connected to the vine by remaining in God's love and being connected to God. Allow Him to live, move and be in your life *(Acts 17:28)* by being His offspring. As an apple tree can not produce pears, make sure the branch of your faith is

90

centered on the right tree. Multiply by being connected to God, and the fruit of your faith will not only sustain and provide for you, but can and will be enjoyed by all those around you.

Tara was a popular girl in class. As I do when students are talking amongst themselves, I try to engage my mind in the tasks at hand and not get involved in conversations unless invited. One day I heard the students discussing Tara. "I hear she's pregnant," one student said. "What?" another guy asked. "Yeah, she stopped wearing tight clothes and she eats a lot at lunch now," the first student repeated. Immediately, students began whispering. "That is not true," one solitary student said with a determinedly final air. "But, how do you know for sure?" "Because I know Tara," he responded. What a powerful testimony that girl had. Her friends knew she was not pregnant because of the strength of her character. I could only hope my friends would think so highly of me.

The Graduate's Blessing

We pray you may imagine all of the possibilities God has for you as you continue on to the next phase of your life. We pray you will make your life full by:

- dividing it into entities of which you can cherish;
- subtracting the unpleasentries of life by trusting in God;
- adding to your faith in order to build a life that counts;
- multiplying by always striving to be a more consummate person.

May the Lord bless you and keep you in sickness and in health, in prosperity and adversity. "May the Lord make His face shine upon you and be gracious to you; the Lord turn his face toward you and give you peace" (*Numbers 6:24-26*).

May you be disciples of Jesus Christ, as you mature and blossom into the wonderful person God has called you to be, in the name of the Father, and of the Son, and of the Holy Spirit. Amen.

Scriptural Index

Colossians 4:6	47
1 Thessalonians 5:2	81
1 Thessalonians 5:17	84
1 Timothy 4:4	6
1 Timothy 4:8	63
2 Timothy 1:5	14
2 Timothy 1:6	72
2 Timothy 4:2	86
2 Timothy 4:5	61
2 Timothy 4:7	39
Titus 3:4-5	55
Philemon 6	88
Hebrews 11:6	52
Hebrews 12:1-2	26
Hebrews 12:29	72
James 1:5	28
James 1:19	47
James 3:2-12	46
James 3:13-18	57
James 4:14	8
1 Peter 1:13	86
1 Peter 4:8	67
1 Peter 5:8	42
2 Peter 1:3	3
2 Peter 1:4	25
2 Peter 1:5	52
2 Peter 1:5-7	51
2 Peter 1:8	71
1 John 3:16	10
Revelation 20:14	72